Contents

A Note to the Student

If you want to communicate with real competence and confidence, you need to develop three editing skills. First, you need to know when you have a potential problem on your hands. (Otherwise, you will never be moved to consult a reference manual; you'll assume that what you have written is correct as it stands.) Second, once you think you have encountered a problem, you need to know where to look for help. Third, once you have found the appropriate rule, you need to know how to apply it correctly to the specific problem you have found.

The *Basic Worksheets,* which accompany the tenth edition of *The Gregg Reference Manual,* have been designed to help you build these three skills. First of all, these worksheets will familiarize you with a wide range of potential problems you are likely to encounter in punctuation, capitalization, number style, abbreviations, plural and possessive forms, spelling, compound words, word division, grammar, and usage (all of which are treated in Sections 1–11 of *The Gregg Reference Manual*). Second, these worksheets will direct you to the basic rules in Sections 1–11 so that later on, when you encounter similar problems in your own work, you'll know where to look. Third, they will sharpen your ability to apply the rules correctly under many different circumstances.

There are 23 worksheets in all. Worksheet 1, the Diagnostic Survey, will show you how much you already know, how good you are at looking things up on your own, and which of the first eleven sections in the manual you need to give special attention to.

Worksheets 2–22 focus on the basic rules within a given section of the manual and also familiarize you with additional rules that represent the application of basic rules to special situations. With the exception of three editing surveys (Worksheets 8, 16, and 22), these worksheets are all organized in the same way. Almost all of the exercises within a given worksheet are each based on a very limited set of rules. The appropriate rule numbers appear next to the answer blanks so that you can quickly find the help you need to resolve the problem at hand. In almost all cases, the exercise items are sequenced according to the numerical order of the rules on which they are based. Thus you can use each exercise within a worksheet as a study guide that will help you master a limited set of rules in each case.

The final exercise in each of these worksheets is an editing exercise that is designed to integrate what you have learned in the process of completing the worksheet. This editing exercise does not indicate which rules apply to the errors you will encounter. Now you will be required to identify the errors on your own and to consult the manual for the guidance you may need.

The three editing surveys (Worksheets 8, 16, and 22) that are interspersed in the sequence also do not provide rule numbers with the exercises. The first editing survey, Worksheet 8, is designed to help you integrate what you have learned about punctuation, capitalization, and number style in the preceding worksheets. There are sentences to be rewritten and editing exercises that require you to draw on the rules you have studied in Sections 1–4 of the manual.

The second editing survey, Worksheet 16, follows the same pattern as Worksheet 8, only now the sentences to be rewritten focus on problems relating to abbreviations, plural and possessive forms, spelling, and compound words (Sections 5–8 in the manual). The two editing exercises will require you to draw on the rules you have studied in Sections 1–9 of the manual.

In the third editing survey, Worksheet 22, the sentences to be rewritten deal with problems of grammar and usage (Sections 10–11). The two editing exercises that follow now require you to draw on the full range of rules you have already worked with in Sections 1–11.

The Final Survey, Worksheet 23, exactly parallels Worksheet 1, the Diagnostic Survey. It will give you the opportunity to demonstrate to your instructor—and, what is more important, to yourself—the considerable gain in skill you have achieved by working your way through these worksheets.

How to Show Corrections. In many of the worksheets you will be asked to identify errors and make corrections within the line (rather than in an answer column). The chart of proofreaders' marks that appears on the inside back cover of *The Gregg Reference Manual* will show you how to indicate various kinds of corrections. Refer to this chart as necessary. (A larger version of this chart appears on pages 358–359 of *The Gregg Reference Manual.*)

 **McGraw-Hill Irwin**

Basic Worksheets to Accompany
THE GREGG REFERENCE MANUAL: A MANUAL OF STYLE, GRAMMAR, USAGE, AND FORMATTING, Tenth Edition
William A. Sabin

Published by McGraw-Hill/Irwin, a business unit of The McGraw-Hill Companies, Inc., 1221 Avenue of the Americas, New York, NY 10020. Copyright © 2005, 2001, 1996, 1992, 1985, 1977, 1970, 1961, 1956, 1951 by The McGraw-Hill Companies, Inc. All rights reserved. No part of this publication may be reproduced or distributed in any form or by any means, or stored in a database or retrieval system, without the prior written consent of The McGraw-Hill Companies, Inc., including, but not limited to, in any network or other electronic storage or transmission, or broadcast for distance learning.

1 2 3 4 5 6 7 8 9 0 QPD/QPD 0 9 8 7 6 5 4

ISBN 0-07-293654-1

www.mhhe.com

The McGraw·Hill Companies

1 Diagnostic Survey

A. Directions: The following items deal with problems of punctuation. Correct all errors by inserting or deleting punctuation, using appropriate proofreaders' marks (shown on pages 358–359 and on the inside back cover of *The Gregg Reference Manual*). Circle any changes you make. If a sentence is correct as given, write *C* in the answer column.
References: Sections 1–2.

1. Will you please indicate your choice below _____

2. Will you please lend me some money _____

3. I asked Jason why he was planning to leave _____

4. Jason, why are you planning to leave _____

5. I hired someone, who is quite experienced. _____

6. It is therefore my intention to resign. _____

7. On Friday May 11 2007 we will be moving to Idaho. _____

8. Bev will be able to help you but Tom and Dwayne are tied up right now. _____

9. My mother my sister and my aunt are planning to attend the wedding. _____

10. It promises to be a cold rainy November. _____

11. To get to our office turn at Exit 54 and go left. _____

12. Before we move in we need to replace the roof and waterproof the basement. _____

13. In my opinion Mr. Honeywell is not giving us the whole story. _____

14. I saw the movie, and agreed with your criticism of the acting. _____

15. Fran loved the show, Hal and I hated it. _____

16. The year 2008 will be our sixtieth year in business. _____

17. The location sounds ideal, for example, your children can walk to school. _____

18. The article called No More Violence appeared in the August issue of *Harper's*. _____

19. What could the word syzygy possibly mean? _____

20. My new cookbook, Stepping Up to the Plate, was published last year. _____

B. Directions: The following items deal with problems of capitalization. If an item is correctly capitalized, write C in the answer column. Correct any incorrect items as follows: To change a capital letter to a small letter, draw a line through it: ~~T~~he. To change a small letter to a capital letter, draw three lines under it: the. Circle any changes you make. **References:** Section 3.

21. were stranded at the O'Hare
    airport _____

22. would like to take a tour of the
    white house _____

23. used to work as a consultant for
    our Company _____

24. once served as Mayor of
    Waldoboro _____

25. wants to ask my Father for
    advice _____

26. because of severe fog at the
    Airport _____

27. somewhere on the west coast—
    maybe Oregon _____

28. dropped out of sight during the
    eighties _____

29. received a Bachelor's degree in
    history _____

30. appears in Chapter 6,
    Page 134 _____

C. Directions: The following items deal with problems of number style and abbreviations. If an item is correct as given, write C in the answer column. If an item is incorrect, circle the error and write the correct form in the answer column. **References:** Sections 4–5.

31. on or before September
    twelfth _____

32. has been reduced by over
    twenty percent _____

33. 38 students and three
    teachers _____

34. sixty-nine thousand
    dollars _____

35. will cost over $500.00 to
    repair _____

36. were sold for only $.30
    apiece _____

37. . . . next month. 6 months
    ago _____

38. toward the end of the
    twentieth century _____

39. will affect over ⅓ of our
    customers _____

40. before we meet at 12:00
    noon _____

41. Jasper A. Throckmorton
    Junior _____

42. revolutions per minute
    (abbreviated) _____

43. will be audited by the
    I.R.S. _____

44. on the basis of your memo.
    of June 4 _____

45. consulted with P.R.
    Voorhees _____

46. get a second opinion from
    Doctor Burgos _____

47. the US Department of
    Education _____

48. no longer lives in
    Washington, D.C. _____

49. 200 gals. *(on an
    invoice)* _____

50. will send the purchase order
    Asap _____

Diagnostic Survey (Continued)

D. Directions: The following items deal with problems of plural and possessive forms, spelling, and compound words. If an item is correct as given, write *C* in the answer column. If an item is incorrect, circle the error and write the correct form in the answer column. **References:** Sections 6–8.

51. made two copys for
    your boss _____

52. met with the three
    attornies _____

53. the rescue squad that
    saved our lifes _____

54. coping with our
    mother-in-laws _____

55. has established only
    one criteria _____

56. have invited a large
    group of VIP's _____

57. has left on a three
    week's trip _____

58. ought to open a
    saving's account _____

59. need to get my boss'
    approval _____

60. bought some
    childrens' toys _____

61. is being transfered
    to Dallas _____

62. don't think it will
    make a difference _____

63. using your best
    judgment _____

64. and recieved it only
    yesterday _____

65. will have to procede
    with Plan B _____

66. which maybe quite
    true _____

67. too much time has
    past _____

68. written on pale blue
    stationary _____

69. will try to
    accomodate you _____

70. asked for seperate
    checks _____

71. need to follow-up
    with Paul _____

72. you can talk to any
    salesman _____

73. double space this
    manuscript _____

74. order something
    more up-to-date _____

75. use our toll free
    number _____

76. considered this to be
    rather old-fashioned _____

77. is well-known for
    her generosity _____

78. counting on your
    co-operation _____

79. was not re-elected
    for another term _____

80. needs to build up his
    self confidence _____

E. Directions: The following items deal with problems of grammar and usage. If an item is correct as given, write *C* in the answer column. If an item is incorrect, circle the error and write the correct form in the answer column. **References:** Sections 10–11.

81. Janice don't seem very happy about her new job. _____

82. One of the printers are broken. _____

83. Joe done it all by himself. _____

84. If I was you, I would not go. _____

85. Dennis and me already have tickets. _____

86. The firm treats it's employees well. _____

87. They've invited Samantha and myself. _____

88. I feel very badly about what I said to Harriet. _____

89. Bo is the best of the two golfers. _____

90. I don't want no one to see this. _____

91. Thanks alot for all that you did. _____

92. I think it happened accidently. _____

93. Do you think this looks alright? _____

94. How will these cutbacks effect our sales? _____

95. A small amount of people responded. _____

96. Drive a little further on. _____

97. Less people came to this week's shows. _____

98. I must of left the report at home. _____

99. We could sure use some help. _____

100. My family use to live in Toledo. _____

4

2 The Period, the Question Mark, and the Exclamation Point

A. Directions: Insert the appropriate mark of punctuation at the end of each sentence and circle it. If a sentence is correct as given, write *C* in the answer column. **References:** Consult the rules shown below as you complete this exercise. See Appendix D for the definition of any grammatical terms that you may not be familiar with.

1. **Statement:** We question the need to reduce the size of the staff at this time	1.	101a
2. **Command:** Send copies to Victoria Hochshield and Jeremy Morgenthal Sr.	2.	101a
3. **Elliptical statement:** Now, to return to the main theme of this presentation	3.	101b
4. **Polite command:** Will you please let me know whether you need more money	4.	103a
5. **Favor:** Will you please let me borrow your BMW this weekend	5.	103b
6. **Indirect question:** I asked Austin why he couldn't play tennis this Saturday	6.	104
7. **Direct question:** Why can't you play tennis this Saturday	7.	110a
8. **Rhetorical question:** Why not come into our store and see for yourself	8.	110b
9. **Elliptical question:** I heard that you're planning to quit. Why	9.	111a
10. **Direct question:** The only question I have is, When will Joe be told	10.	115 / 104
11. **Indirect question:** The only question I have is when Joe will be told	11.	115
12. **Exclamations:** Wow I think what you did was fantastic	12.	119a

B. Directions: Insert the appropriate mark of punctuation at the end of each sentence and circle it. If a sentence is correct as given, write *C* in the answer column. **References:** Consult the rules shown below as you complete this exercise.

13. Do not speak to anyone from MacroTechnology Inc.	13.	101a
14. I doubt whether I'll be able to take any time off in July	14.	101a
15. You wanted to know whether we are still accepting applications Of course	15.	101a–b
16. May I suggest that you send your résumé directly to Mrs. Hoehn	16.	103a
17. Will you please call me if you have any further questions	17.	103a
18. May I get an advance copy of the report you are preparing for your boss	18.	103b
19. May I ask your assistant for help while mine is on vacation	19.	103b
20. Why Tina stormed out of here is something I can't explain	20.	104
21. You asked whether you could take Friday off By all means	21.	104 / 101b
22. Do you have any contacts at Cybernautics Inc.	22.	110a
23. Why not take advantage of this money-back guarantee	23.	110b
24. Why bother I don't think there's any point in discussing this further	24.	111a / 101a
25. We won We beat them by just one point It's unbelievable	25.	119a

C. Directions: Insert punctuation as necessary in the following items, and circle any changes you make. If an item is correct as given, write *C* in the answer column. **References:** ¶¶106–107.

26. This technical writing program will help you:

 a Analyze the purpose and the audience for your writing

 b Develop and organize the content

 c Edit for clarity and accuracy   26. _____ 106 107a

27. We can help you improve your sales and marketing operations with the following

 custom-designed software:

 • Customer information system

 • Product information system

 • Competitive information system   27. _____ 106 107b

D. Directions: Rewrite the following sentences to correct all errors in punctuation. Eliminate sentence fragments and adjust the capitalization as necessary. **References:** Consult the rules shown below as you complete this exercise.

28. Have you heard the latest. Our firm is merging with Sigma Inc.. I still don't believe it. _____ 110a 101a 119a

 _____

29. I plan to buy a new SUV. As soon as I find a better job that pays more. _____ 101c

 _____

30. Will you let us use your swimming pool? While you're away. _____ 101c 103b

 _____

31. We would like to ask when you are coming to Omaha? Could you stay with us? For a few days. 104 101c 110a

 _____

32. The big question now is how will we break the news to your parents. _____ 115

 _____

E. Directions: Edit the following paragraph to correct all errors in punctuation. Eliminate sentence fragments and adjust the capitalization as necessary. Use appropriate proofreaders' marks (shown on pages 358–359 and on the inside back cover of *The Gregg Reference Manual*) to indicate your corrections. For example, to change a capital letter to a small letter, draw a line through it: *The*. Circle any changes you make. **References:** Consult the appropriate rules in ¶¶101–119.

```
        Is it true?  That you sold your house and will be moving up to your cottage          1

at the lake.  Great news.  Janet and I have been talking about whether we should            2

do the same thing?  We realize that we can't afford to move.  Until we sell the             3

house we live in now.  We have no idea how much our house is worth.  Would you              4

please tell us how much you got for your house.  We would also appreciate                   5

learning something about:                                                                   6

    1.  The real estate agent who handled the sale for you                                  7

    2.  Our new neighbors                                                                   8

    3.  The availability of affordable housing up at the lake                               9

In any event, congratulations!  When can we get you two over to celebrate.                 10
```

6

3 The Comma

A. Directions: Insert commas as necessary in the following sentences, and circle any changes you make. If a sentence is correct as given, write *C* in the answer column. **References:** Read ¶122, especially the introductory note. See Appendix D for the definition of any grammatical terms that you may not be familiar with.

1. **Nonessential expression:** I hired Tom Rae who has a lot of experience.   1. _____ 122
2. **Essential expression:** I hired someone who has a lot of experience.   2. _____ 122
3. **Nonessential expression:** We have decided therefore not to accept your offer.   3. _____ 122
4. **Essential expression:** We have therefore decided not to accept your offer.   4. _____ 122
5. **Interrupting expression:** Let's meet on Friday or if you wish on Monday.   5. _____ 122a
6. **Afterthought:** You still haven't made your mind up have you?   6. _____ 122b
7. **Transitional expression:** It is true nevertheless that Bob's work is good.   7. _____ 122c
8. **Transitional expression:** It is nevertheless true that Bob's work is good.   8. _____ 122c
9. **Independent comment:** It is certainly our intention to act quickly.   9. _____ 122c
10. **Independent comment:** It is our intention certainly to act quickly.   10. _____ 122c
11. **Descriptive expression:** Thanks for the memo of May 2 in which you . . .   11. _____ 122d
12. **Descriptive expression:** Thanks for the memo in which you . . .   12. _____ 122d
13. **Date:** The concert has been rescheduled for Friday July 6 2007 at 8 p.m.   13. _____ 122e
14. **Names:** Helen Moraga M.D. is moving her practice to Bath Maine in May.   14. _____ 122f
15. **Names (preferences unknown):** John Blake Jr. is joining Pennon Inc.   15. _____ 122f

B. Directions: Insert commas as necessary in the following sentences, and circle any changes you make. If a sentence is correct as given, write *C* in the answer column. **References:** ¶122.

16. Let's interview Simon Perry who worked in this department for over three years.   16. _____ 122
17. It is therefore essential that we investigate this complaint at once.   17. _____ 122
18. It is essential therefore that we investigate this complaint at once.   18. _____ 122
19. It is true isn't it that Marcia will be promoted rather than Tanya?   19. _____ 122a
20. Helen Wu resigned as company treasurer last June if I remember correctly.   20. _____ 122b
21. You must remember however that this situation is only temporary.   21. _____ 122c
22. Our investors in my opinion will not be satisfied with our year-end results.   22. _____ 122c
23. Thank you for your letter of July 9 in which you asked about our discounts.   23. _____ 122d
24. The Board of Directors will meet on Monday August 6 2007 at 10 a.m.   24. _____ 122e
25. Warren Himmelfarb Ph.D. of Medina Ohio will teach this seminar next year.   25. _____ 122f

C. Directions: Insert commas as necessary in the following sentences, and circle any changes you make. If a sentence is correct as given, write *C* in the answer column. **References:** ¶¶123–124.

26. **Compound sentence:** I can't meet this Friday but I'm free next week. 26. _____ 123a
27. **Series:** I've asked Gloria Ted and Alison to work on this project with me. 27. _____ 123b
28. **Adjectives:** This tough job calls for a cool low-key person. 28. _____ 123c
29. **Numbers:** Homes like this cost between $800000 and $1200000. 29. _____ 123d
30. **Clarity:** Why the production schedule fell apart I can't explain. 30. _____ 123e
31. **Introductory word:** Well we all make mistakes like that. 31. _____ 124
32. **Introductory phrase:** To understand why the schedule slipped ask Tim. 32. _____ 124
33. **Introductory clause:** After the dust settles find out what happened. 33. _____ 124
34. **Introductory adverb:** Yesterday we spent the day reviewing budgets. 34. _____ 124b
35. **Introductory phrase:** In the afternoon we'll have more time to talk. 35. _____ 124b
36. **Transitional expression:** In any case it's too late to change course. 36. _____ 124b
37. **Independent comment:** In my judgment we should not say anything more. 37. _____ 124b

D. Directions: Insert commas as necessary in the following sentences, and circle any changes you make. If a sentence is correct as given, write *C* in the answer column. **References:** ¶¶123–124.

38. I've spoken to Amy and Dave but I can't reach Mike Betty or Dru. 38. _____ 123a 123b
39. We could use a restful vacation after our long hard winter. 39. _____ 123c
40. How I lost $40000 on that investment I'll never understand. 40. _____ 123d 123e
41. Yes I can readily understand why you feel as you do. 41. _____ 124
42. To learn more about this offer call 1.800.555.3261. 42. _____ 124
43. As soon as our CEO returns we should be able to resolve this problem. 43. _____ 124
44. On the weekend I may be able to start painting our bedroom. 44. _____ 124b
45. On the other hand I may want to go skiing at Devil's Gorge. 45. _____ 124b

E. Directions: Edit the following paragraph to correct all errors in the use of commas. Use appropriate proofreaders' marks (shown on pages 358–359 and on the inside back cover of *The Gregg Reference Manual*) to indicate your corrections. Circle any changes you make. **References:** ¶¶122–124.

```
Well guess who got stuck with organizing Henry Richmond's retirement        1
party?  I don't know why I was chosen but I know that I can't handle it      2
myself.  That's why I'm asking for help from colleagues, who have had        3
experience in managing such affairs.  To get to the point I hope that you,   4
Fred Fox, and Nan Shea will agree to share the joy, the honor and the burden 5
of working with me on this event.  If we all pitch in the planning should go 6
smoothly.  The problem however is that we don't have much time.  It is,      7
therefore, critical that we meet tomorrow to agree on a distribution of      8
labor.  In my opinion you would be the best person to organize the          9
presentations.  Given your warm ingratiating manner, you should have no     10
trouble lining people up.                                                   11
```

8

4

The Comma (Continued)

A. Directions: Correct the following sentences by inserting missing commas, striking out inappropriate commas, and supplying any other punctuation that may be needed. Circle any changes you make. If a sentence is correct as given, write *C* in the answer column. **References:** Consult the rules shown below as you complete this exercise. For the definition of any grammatical terms that you may not be familiar with, see Appendix D.

1. **Compound sentence:** I finished the Garvey ads last week and I am now working on Garvey's catalog.

    1.   126a 127a

2. **Compound predicate:** I finished the Garvey ads last week, and am now working on Garvey's catalog.

    2.   127b

3. **Run-on sentence:** I finished the Garvey ads last week, I am now working on Garvey's catalog.

    3.   128

4. **Compound sentence:** Please call Brian and ask whether he is free for lunch next Monday.

    4.   127c 129

5. **Introductory dependent clause:** Before you watch the videotape you should scan the script.

    5.   130a

6. **Essential dependent clause:** We need updated sales data when we meet with the managers.

    6.   131a

7. **Nonessential dependent clause:** We need updated sales data by Monday when we meet with the managers.

    7.   131b

8. **Nonessential dependent clause:** I want to explore the ancient ruins of Greece for I have a deep interest in archaeology.

    8.   131b 132

9. **Introductory phrase:** In 2008 my wife and I will celebrate our fortieth wedding anniversary.

    9.   135c

10. **Introductory phrase:** In reviewing your application I noticed a few significant omissions.

    10.   135c

B. Directions: Correct the following sentences by inserting missing commas, striking out inappropriate commas, and supplying any other punctuation that may be needed. Circle any changes you make. If a sentence is correct as given, write *C* in the answer column. **References:** Consult the rules shown below as you complete this exercise.

11. Either we cut our prices sharply or we watch our competitors steal our customers.

    11.   126a 127a

12. Not only was the pianist excellent but the orchestra was in fine form as well.

    12.   126a 127a

13. Paul passed his California bar exams last month, and is now practicing in Palo Alto.

    13.   127b

Name   Date   Class   9

14. Bert will write the in-house announcement, I will handle the press release and the media interviews.

14. _____ 128

15. Check with Sheila, and see what she thinks about the plan.

15. _____ 127c
_____ 129

16. If Sid can't join us on Saturday ask whether he can send someone in his place.

16. _____ 130a

17. If possible let us have your decision on the revised contract terms by next Wednesday.

17. _____ 130b

18. The person, who sold us that equipment, no longer works for FaxCo.

18. _____ 131a

19. Vera Suggs, who sold us that equipment, no longer works for FaxCo.

19. _____ 131b

20. I would not recommend Doug for that job even though I like him personally.

20. _____ 131b
_____ 132

21. Having watched you build the business from scratch I'm truly proud of your success.

21. _____ 135a

22. To understand what Steve is recommending you have to read his full report.

22. _____ 135b

23. At the time the hearing was going on Bob was still churning out new data.

23. _____ 135c

24. Our efforts, to increase our market share, are working quite well.

24. _____ 137a

25. Our main goal this year, to increase our market share, will be achieved.

25. _____ 137b

C. **Directions:** Insert commas as necessary in the following items, and circle any changes you make. If an item is correct as given, write *C* in the answer column. **References:** Consult the rules shown below as you complete this exercise.

26. In short I think we should cancel the program in spite of the time and money already invested.

26. _____ 138a
_____ 139a

27. Thus I felt it was pointless to try to reconcile my differences with Don Springer.

27. _____ 139b

28. You asked whether I thought you were qualified to take over the opening in Finance. Of course you are.

28. _____ 139c

29. Sales and profits should begin to pick up in the fourth quarter in my opinion.

29. _____ 140

30. It is certainly true that the manager of the Purchasing Department should have used better judgment.

30. _____ 141

31. It is true certainly that the manager of the Purchasing Department should have used better judgment.

31. _____ 141

32. I had hoped to get more money for our house; however let's accept the best offer that we get in the next month.

32. _____ 142a

33. If we receive your contest entry form by March 31, you can be a winner too.

33. _____ 130a
_____ 143a

10

The Comma (Continued)

34. You too can be a winner if we receive your contest entry by March 31.

35. The corporation purchased the Goldmark estate in 1994 for $2,500,000 if I remember correctly.

36. Joe along with Sybil and Ned is setting up a training program to help managers make better use of their computers.

37. Greta rather than Hal will be representing the company at the small business conference in Washington.

38. On Friday August 12 we are starting off on a tour of Europe.

39. The term *muffin-choker* refers to a bizarre item that you read in the morning paper as you eat your breakfast.

40. The book *Networking to the Top* sold over 50,000 copies in the first month of publication.

41. Jake's new book *Networking to the Top* sold over 50,000 copies in the first month of publication.

42. My husband, Ralph, feels that our business would do much better if we moved to southern California.

43. My older sister Fay Boyarski says that Ralph is much too pessimistic about business conditions here on the East Coast.

44. I myself felt that you did the right thing by refusing to modify your recommendations.

45. Many thanks for your memo of May 2 in which you offered to cover for Tony Parsons while he was on paternity leave.

34.	143b
35.	144a
36.	146a
37.	147
38.	148
39.	149
40.	149
41.	149
42.	150
43.	150
44.	150
45.	152

D. Directions: Insert commas as necessary in the following items, and circle any changes you make. If an item is correct as given, write *C* in the answer column. **References:** Consult the rules shown below as you complete this exercise.

46. After December 31 2007 please use the new address and telephone number shown on the enclosed card.

47. On Friday February 23 2007 I plan to give notice of my intention to resign and return to college for an advanced degree.

48. The May 2008 issue of *The Atlantic Monthly* contains an article on how to consolidate school districts to make them more cost-effective.

49. Did you know that Ronald Foley Jr. *(style preference unknown)* has been made a senior vice president?

50. Phyllis Horowitz Ph.D. will be the main speaker at a program designed for direct marketing consultants.

46.	154a
47.	154b
48.	155a
49.	156
50.	157

51. Writen Inc. *(style preference unknown)* announced today that it would
    move its headquarters back to New York City.   51. _____159_____

52. I'm planning to move from Klein Texas to Xenia Ohio.   52. _____160a_____

53. We offer a number of different product lines for children teenagers and
    adults.   53. _____162a_____

54. I've been told that Vail Fox & Bly *(style preference unknown)* is an
    excellent law firm.   54. _____163_____

55. Computer terms such as *bug, glitch,* and so on are often . . .   55. _____164_____

56. Coffee, tea, and soda, are the only things I plan to serve.   56. _____165_____

57. The same error appears in all of our ads and brochures and catalogs
    released this month.   57. _____166_____

58. A town meeting on the topic of weeknight curfews should be of great
    interest to teenagers, and adults.   58. _____167_____

59. You have prepared an effective well-written report.   59. _____168a_____

60. You have prepared an effective annual report.   60. _____169_____

61. A number of important new Supreme Court decisions were handed down
    at the end of this year's session.   61. _____170_____

62. You'll have to negotiate a narrow, twisting, two-lane, road in order to
    reach our house.   62. _____171_____

63. The fact is we have many more competitors than we used to.   63. _____172b_____

64. First come first served.   64. _____123e_____
                                                                                      _____172d_____

65. Now now don't worry about it.   65. _____175c_____

E. Directions: Edit the following paragraph to correct all errors in the use of commas. Use appropriate proofreaders' marks (shown on pages 358–359 and on the inside back cover of *The Gregg Reference Manual*) to indicate your corrections. Circle any changes you make. **References:** Consult the appropriate rules in ¶¶126–175 as you complete this exercise.

```
    Next Friday July 18 my wife, Sally, and I are starting a          1
two-week bicycle tour through New England. We will be part of a        2
group tour but the tour offers us some private time and some           3
personal flexibility, too. The company, that runs the tour, has        4
booked us into charming, country inns each night. Moreover our         5
daily cycling itinerary brings us to points of historical in-          6
terest, and allows time for frequent rest stops, picnic lunches        7
and gourmet snacks. The feature of the tour that I like best is        8
the van that accompanies us wherever we pedal. Whenever my             9
energy gives out I know the van will carry me and my bicycle to       10
the next stop on the tour.                                            11
```

Other Marks of Punctuation

A. Directions: Each of the following sentences consists of *two independent clauses.* Insert a semicolon, colon, or period between the clauses. Change the capitalization as necessary. Circle any changes you make. **References:** ¶¶176, 187. See Appendix D for the definition of any grammatical terms that you may not be familiar with.

1. My partner wants us to open a second store this year I think that would be a big mistake.

   176a

2. Many thanks for your memo of July 2 the data you requested can be assembled in less than a week.

   176b

3. Your new cottage sounds perfect it's right on the lake and has a private room and bath just for me.

   187a–c

4. Your new cottage sounds perfect mine is not on the lake and has no extra rooms for guests.

   187b–c

5. Your new cottage sounds perfect for example, the lakeside location is ideal for swimming, boating, and ice skating.

   187b–c

B. Directions: Each of the following sentences contains a **boldface** phrase or clause. Correct the punctuation before, after, and within each boldface expression, and change the capitalization as necessary. Circle any changes you make. **References:** Consult the rules shown below as you complete this exercise.

6. I think we should take my father to a doctor **however my brother thinks that we should not interfere.**

   178

7. My sisters agree with my brother **hence I have said nothing more about my concerns.**

   178

8. The offer from Bromley & Finch is quite attractive **for example they are willing to meet our price.**

   178
   181a

9. I have only one other question **namely how quickly can we transfer ownership?**

   178
   181b
   188

10. Do not use periods in acronyms **for example NASDAQ (not N.A.S.D.A.Q.).**

    178
    182a

11. There is only one more step we need to take **namely get my boss to okay the terms of the contract.**

    178
    182b

12. In my office we transfer electronic data by means of *sneakernet* **that is by carrying a diskette from one computer to another.**

    178
    182c

13. Some of our suppliers **for example Wynn** may be raising prices soon. *(No special treatment required.)*

    178
    183

14. Some of our suppliers **for example, Wynn, Place, and Shaw** may be raising prices soon. *(Emphasize phrase.)*

    183
    202

Name _____ Date _____ Class _____

15. Some of our suppliers **for example, Wynn, Place, and Shaw** may be raising prices soon. *(De-emphasize phrase.)*

    183
    219b

16. Replacement parts for this equipment are manufactured only in our **Carbondale Pennsylvania** factory.

    219a

17. Please send us **1) your résumé, 2) samples of your work, and 3) a list of references we can contact.**

    222a

18. Please call me by **Friday, (October 3)** if you want us to proceed with the market research.

    224a
    221
    225a–c

19. You will find a detailed analysis of this topic in **Chapter 4 (see pages 98–112.).**

    220

20. You will find a detailed analysis of this topic in **Chapter 4. (See pages 98–112).**

    226
    220

C. Directions: In each of the following sentences, correct the capitalization of the word following the colon as necessary. Use appropriate proofreaders' marks (shown on pages 358–359 and on the inside back cover of *The Gregg Reference Manual*) to indicate your corrections. Circle any changes you make. If a sentence is correct as given, write *C* in the answer column. **References:** Consult the rules shown below as you complete this exercise.

21. You need the following qualifications for this job: A college degree and some retailing experience.

21. _____ 196

22. I think Nan should head the group: She's good with people and she understands the key issues.

22. _____ 197

23. My china shop operates on a simple principle: If you break it, you've bought it.

23. _____ 198

24. Please keep the following things in mind: a project of this size will have a lot of last-minute details. There will not be enough "last minutes" in which to deal with them.

24. _____ 199a

25. Caution: do not enter this room when a red light is flashing.

25. _____ 199d

D. Directions: Correct the punctuation before, after, and within the boldface elements in the following sentences. Change the capitalization as necessary. Use appropriate revision marks to indicate your corrections. Circle any changes you make. If a sentence is correct as given, write *C* in the answer column. **References:** Consult the rules shown below as you complete this exercise.

26. **Direct quote:** Mr. Potter said, **I want it done. And I want it done now.**

26. _____ 227

27. **Indirect quote:** Mr. Potter said that **"he wanted action taken immediately."**

27. _____ 228a

28. **Article title:** I've just submitted an article entitled **Finding a Job in Today's Market.**

28. _____ 240a
    242

29. **"So-called" expression:** If you consider the reduced size of the new box, their **so-called "price cut"** is really a price increase.

29. _____ 240b

14

Other Marks of Punctuation (Continued)

30. Quoted statement: **Let's call Sam Hathaway and get his advice.** Jerry suggested.

     30. _____ 253a / 247a

31. Quoted question: **Why should we consider such a disappointing offer,** Marian asked?

     31. _____ 254 / 249a

32. Quoted statement: Mr. Kelly's previous boss said **He's a lot smarter than he looks.**

     32. _____ 256a / 247a

33. Quoted question: The defense attorney asked **What is your evidence for this accusation.**

     33. _____ 256a / 249a

34. Quoted statement: Did Louise really say **I'm going to hand in my resignation.**

     34. _____ 256a / 249b

35. Quoted statements: Here's what Louise actually said, **I've made up my mind. I won't work for that bozo.**

     35. _____ 256b–c / 247a

E. Directions: Insert underlining or quotation marks as appropriate for the boldface expressions in the following sentences. Use appropriate proofreaders' marks to indicate your corrections. Circle any changes you make. If a sentence is correct as given, write *C* in the answer column. **References:** Consult the rules shown below as you complete this exercise.

36. What do the words **newbie** and **newsgroup** mean?

     36. _____ 285a

37. The Germans would use the word **gemütlich** to describe the atmosphere of this restaurant.

     37. _____ 287

38. Richard, my nerdy brother, is graduating **summa cum laude** from the University of North Dakota.

     38. _____ 287

39. You'll enjoy an article entitled **Human Rights for Motorists** in a recent issue of **BusinessWeek**.

     39. _____ 242 / 289a

40. I urge you to read this book: **Electronic Networks: A Surfer's Guide, Second Edition.**

     40. _____ 289a, f

41. What does the phrase **surfing the Net** actually mean?

     41. _____ 290a, c

42. I always seem to make a mistake when I try to use **affect** or **effect**.

     42. _____ 285a / 290c

43. How would you define the terms **landscape orientation** and **portrait orientation**?

     43. _____ 285a / 290a, c

44. Have you read **Newsweek's** article on the influence of corporate lobbyists on federal legislation?

     44. _____ 289a / 290d

45. I think his writing contains too many **howevers** and not enough **therefores**.

     45. _____ 290d

I've been collecting material about new computer terms for
some time. Writing a book rather than an article on this subject appeals to me for two reasons: 1) 1 already have enough
material for a book. (2) 1 could use the extra space to analyze
the people who dream up these terms. I wouldn't bother with
ordinary words like "bit" and "byte." The kinds of words I have
in mind, for example, *notwork, vaporware,* and *sneakernet,* re-
flect the wacky, offbeat humor of computer programmers and
users. (In case you're interested, *notwork* refers to a network
that does not live up to its advance billing, *vaporware* refers
to software that is being heavily promoted, even though it has
serious developmental problems that could doom its eventual
release). I would also deal with abbreviations that have ac-
quired crazy pronunciations. For example, SCSI (Pronounced
scuzzy). I've sent a proposal to a San Mateo, California,
publishing house that issued a successful book entitled
"The Internet for Dummies." Maybe the editors will see
another winner in my idea.

1
2
3
4
5
6
7
8
9
10
11
12
13
14
15
16
17
18

6 Capitalization

A. Directions: Correct the capitalization as necessary in each of the following items. Use appropriate proofreaders' marks (shown on pages 358–359 and on the inside back cover of *The Gregg Reference Manual*) to indicate your corrections. Circle any changes you make. If an item is correct as given, write *C* in the answer column. **References:** Consult the rules shown below as you complete this exercise. See Appendix D for the definition of any grammatical terms that you may not be familiar with.

1.	your news is great! congratulations!	301a 301b	11.	our Company	308
2.	Jen then asked, "who cares?"	301c	12.	the Post Office	309a
3.	The question is, who will do it?	301d	13.	Fifth and Sixth avenues	309a
4.	the red cross	303	14.	Danish pastry	309b 312a
5.	the internet	303	15.	Governor-Elect Paderewski	317
6.	The Statue of Liberty	303	16.	as president of the United States	312b
7.	a congressional hearing	304	17.	the governor of Virginia	313b
8.	a good samaritan	305	18.	the Mayor of their town	313c
9.	roman numerals	306	19.	let's talk to Mother about it	318
10.	a few Senators	307	20.	let's talk to my Mother about it	319a

B. Directions: Correct the capitalization as necessary in each of the following items. Use appropriate proofreaders' marks to indicate your corrections. Circle any changes you make. If an item is correct as given, write *C* in the answer column. **References:** Consult the rules shown below as you complete this exercise.

21.	the Kmart corporation	320a	36.	the fourth of July	342
22.	this corporation	321	37.	the American revolution	344a
23.	The House of Representatives	325	38.	the Space Age	344b
24.	our local Police Department	327	39.	throughout the Nineties	345
25.	Federal tax regulations	328	40.	took the fifth amendment	346a
26.	every state in the union	330a	41.	medicare patients	347a
27.	the Hotel *(referring to the Plaza)*	331	42.	native Americans	348a
28.	moved to the big apple	333a	43.	God in his glory	349b
29.	the City of Fort Lauderdale	334	44.	the ten commandments	350a
30.	the state of North Carolina	335a	45.	come down to Earth	351
31.	moved to the west coast	338a	46.	two courses in Economics	352
32.	the west coast of the island	338b	47.	a Bachelor's degree	353
33.	Southern politicians	340	48.	met at the Laundromat	356a
34.	the Southern half of Idaho	340	49.	chapter 6	359
35.	northern New Hampshire	341	50.	won the Nobel prize	364

C. Directions: Correct the capitalization of the boldface elements as necessary in the following sentences. Use appropriate proofreaders' marks to indicate your corrections. Circle any changes you make. If a sentence is correct as given, write *C* in the answer column. **References:** Consult the rules shown below as you complete this exercise.

51. **From a company memo:** When we next meet, we need to:
    - **invite the general managers** to talk about their goals.
    - **review the Company's** commitment to the **City's** redevelopment
      plans.
    - **discuss** our upcoming presentation to **the board of directors.**

    51. _____
    301e
    313d
    321
    334
    322

52. Call the **Marketing Director** of Worknet—**Her** name is Amy Fong, I believe—and
    ask about her experience with **Powerpoint.**

    52. _____
    313d-e
    302a
    366a

53. Bernard Lisker, the **President** of our **Company,** is attending a **white house**
    conference on the role of the **Federal Government** in international trade.

    53. _____
    313a
    308
    305
    329

54. Let's ask the **Doctor** if **Penicillin** would stop this infection.

    54. _____
    308
    356

55. Last **Fall,** at the start of my **Junior** year, I decided to major in **Art.**

    55. _____
    343
    354
    352

56. **An article title:** "**The new tax bill: is it to be a bonanza or a disaster?**"

    56. _____
    360
    361

57. **An article title:** "**a follow-up on e-mail—how to make it work for you.**"

    57. _____
    360a-b
    361
    363

58. I applied for the job of **Programmer** in their **systems department.**

    58. _____
    313e
    322

59. This booklet **(See Pages 16–18)** discusses **Social Security benefits.**

    59. _____
    302a
    359
    347a

60. Enclosed is a **xerox** copy of a list of **realtors** from the **yellow pages.**

    60. _____
    356

D. Directions: Edit the following paragraph to correct all capitalization errors. Use appropriate proofreaders' marks to indicate your corrections. Circle any changes you make. **References:** Consult the appropriate rules in Section 3 as you complete this exercise.

```
Early last Winter, in the middle of my junior year in college, the pro-        1
fessor who taught my Political Science seminar invited me to help him with a    2
book he is writing. The assignment has required me to gather information from   3
key officials in the federal government as well as from the Governors from      4
every State in the Union. We are trying to assess the financial impact of       5
Federal environmental protection laws on the states in the course of the        6
Twenty-First Century. My Father is quite proud of what I'm doing. He keeps      7
asking me, "when are you going to Washington to interview the president?" I      8
keep reminding him that I am only the Research Assistant and not the author.    9
```

7 Numbers

A. Directions: Circle all errors in number style in each of the following items, and write the correct form in the answer column. Follow the *figure style.* If an item is correct as given, write *C* in the answer column. **References:** ¶¶401–403.

1. eight messages	401a	11. a 6-month research study		401b
2. about twelve phone calls	401a	12. found on page eight		401b
3. over two thousand words	401a	13. a 5-year loan		401b
4. April fourth	401b	14. over 20 years ago		401d
5. seven dollars	401b	15. 6 people showed up.		401d
6. nine a.m.	401b	16. our 15th anniversary		401d
7. a score of seven to six	401b	17. one-fourth of my income		401d
8. got a sixty on the exam	401b	18. six men and 10 women		402
9. four percent	401b	19. six men and 12 women		402
10. six ft	401b	20. four million dollars		403a

B. Directions: Circle all errors in number style in each of the following items, and write the correct form in the answer column. Follow the *word style.* If an item is correct as given, write *C* in the answer column. **References:** ¶¶404–406.

21. 12 e-mail messages	404a	26. 126 yeses and forty nos		405
22. more than 50 visitors	404a	27. 200 yeses and 145 nos		405
23. at least 75 friends	404a	28. two million years ago		406
24. over 500 get-well cards	404a	29. two and a half million		406
25. over 550 get-well cards	404a	30. 20,000,000		406

C. Directions: Circle all errors in number style and related punctuation in each of the following items, and write the correct form in the answer column. Follow the *figure style* unless another style is called for. If an item is correct as given, write *C* in the answer column. **References:** Consult the rules shown below as you complete this exercise.

31. **Formal style:** the 3d of May	407a	36. twenty thousand dollars		413a
32. **Emphatic style:** the 3d of May	407a	37. bills for $27.00 and $49.50		415
33. June eighth	407b	38. $2 to $4 million		416d
34. the tenth of August, 2007	408d	39. costs only $.25		418a
35. the October, 2006, issue	410	40. $2 million to 4 million		419

D. Directions: Circle all errors in number style in each of the following items, and write the correct form in the answer column. Follow the *figure style* unless another style is called for. If an item is correct as given, write *C* in the answer column. **References:** Consult the rules shown below as you complete this exercise.

41. . . . now. 6 to 12 years ago	421	43. in the 1st century		424
42. several 1000 brochures	423	44. two-thirds of the voters		427a

Name _____ Date _____ Class _____   19

45.	a ½ hour later	_____ 427a	48.	pensions at the age of 60	_____ 433
46.	**Technical style:** six feet	_____ 429a	49.	my four-year-old niece	_____ 434
47.	**Technical style:** 9´ × 12´	_____ 432	50.	on my 50th birthday	_____ 435

E. Directions: Circle all errors in number style and related punctuation in each of the following items, and write the correct form in the answer column. Follow the *figure style* unless another style is called for. If an item is correct as given, write *C* in the answer column. **References:** Consult the rules shown below as you complete this exercise.

51.	a bill payable in 3 months	_____ 436a	59.	30–40%	_____ 453b
52.	vacation 2 weeks from now	_____ 437 / 424	60.	in 2002 16 new outlets	_____ 456
53.	20th-century music	_____ 438	61.	250 8-page brochures	_____ 457
54.	during the 90's	_____ 439a	62.	37500 units in stock	_____ 461a
55.	opens at nine a.m.	_____ 440a	63.	3,905 Morgan Street	_____ 462
56.	closes at 5:00 p.m.	_____ 440c	64.	**Word style:** 51,000	_____ 465
57.	**Emphatic style:** six o'clock	_____ 441a	65.	**Word style:** 1100	_____ 466
58.	only one percent	_____ 447a	66.	a wad of twentys	_____ 467

F. Directions: Rewrite the following sentences to correct any errors in number style and related punctuation. Follow the *figure style.* **References:** Consult the appropriate rules in Section 4 as you complete this exercise.

67. On March 8th, 1993 we were married. In 2008, we will celebrate our 15th anniversary. _____ 408a / 410 / 424

_____

68. The January, 2008, issue of *Workaholic* describes the routines of fourteen women, ten men, and one married couple. _____ 410 / 402

_____

69. 15 to 20 percent of the students we interviewed said that they rarely did more than ½ hour of homework each night. _____ 421 / 427a / 410

_____

70. On April 15 eighteen callers expressed interest in our offer to sell a few 100 acres. _____ 456 / 401a / 423

_____

G. Directions: Edit the following paragraph to correct any errors in number style and related punctuation. Follow the *figure style.* If a figure needs to be in words, supply the spelled-out form. Use appropriate proofreaders' marks (shown on pages 358–359 and on the inside back cover of *The Gregg Reference Manual*) to indicate your corrections. Circle any changes you make. **References:** Consult the appropriate rules in Section 4 as you complete this exercise.

```
    On my 21st birthday, March fifth, I will inherit several 1000 dollars        1

from the estate of my grandfather, who died 4 years ago.  I plan to use fifty    2

percent of my inheritance to pay off part of my tuition loans.  2 months from    3

now, with the other 1/2 of my inheritance, I may take a tour that covers 6       4

countries in four weeks and costs between $2,000 and 3000.  If my inheritance    5

is over $10,000, I may buy a new car instead.                                    6
```

8

Editing Survey A

A. Directions: Rewrite the following sentences to correct all errors in punctuation, capitalization, and number style. Follow the *figure style* for numbers. **References:** Consult the appropriate rules in Sections 1–4 as you complete this exercise.

1. Our Company is expanding its export business, and will be opening new, shipping facilities in Portland, Oregon on July first.

   _____

   _____

   _____

2. Would you please let my son borrow your van. He needs to bring about twelve boxes of books and clothes home from College.

   _____

   _____

   _____

3. In 2006, our company published between ten and 15 books on the subject of Computer Technology. Don't you think that's rather impressive.

   _____

   _____

   _____

4. My Mother and my sister, Anne, opened their consulting business on January 31, 2005. A date that none of us in the family will ever forget.

   _____

   _____

   _____

5. I would like to ask whether it is legally permissible for me to xerox eighty-five copies of an article entitled *Ethical Considerations in Business Decisions?*

   _____

   _____

   _____

6. This request for a ten percent salary increase will have to be approved by 1) the general manager, 2) the director of finance and 3) the President.

_____

_____

_____

7. 24 people responded to our ad for a room clerk but more than ¾ of the applicants had no previous Hotel experience. Unbelievable

_____

_____

_____

8. Thank you for your letter of March 9th in which you asked for the location of our branch offices in the State of Maryland.

_____

_____

_____

9. For a good analysis of business trends in the 90's read chapter 7 (See page 121 in particular.) in a book entitled "The Outlook for Emerging Markets".

_____

_____

_____

10. It is, nevertheless, true that we are facing an $80000 shortfall in sales this Summer, therefore I am scheduling a managers' meeting for nine a.m. tomorrow.

_____

_____

_____

Editing Survey A (Continued)

B. Directions: Edit the following paragraphs to correct all errors in punctuation, capitalization, and number style. Follow the *figure style* for numbers. Use appropriate proofreaders' marks (shown on pages 358–359 and on the inside back cover of *The Gregg Reference Manual*) to indicate your corrections. Circle any changes you make. **References:** Consult the appropriate rules in Sections 1–4 as you complete this exercise.

```
        Are you one of those people who think that all New Yorkers       1

are cold hostile people. Well, it may not be true. The New York          2

Times recently carried a story about a doctor who was living in          3

Manhattan and practicing across the river in New Jersey. On a            4

bitterly cold, Winter morning, he discovered that his car                5

(parked on the street overnight) would not start. "How will I            6

get to my morning appointments?" he wondered.                            7

        As he sat there, another New Yorker hovered alongside in         8

his car, waiting for the doctor to give up his parking space.            9

After one more futile attempt to start the car the doctor got           10

out and told the waiting driver to look for another parking             11

space. Then he went on to say, "I have an even bigger                    12

problem. I don't know how I'm going to get to my patients               13

in New Jersey today."                                                   14

        The hovering driver asked, "What time do you get back           15

to your apartment here in the City"?                                    16

        "Oh, about 5:30," said the doctor.                              17

        "Look," said the driver. "You don't have a car. I don't         18

have a parking space. Take my car today. You can return it              19

to me right here about 5:30 this afternoon."                            20

        The doctor and the driver shook hands on the deal, and          21

went their separate ways. What do you think of that?                    22
```

C. Directions: Edit the following paragraphs to correct all errors in punctuation, capitalization, and number style. Follow the *figure style* for numbers. Use appropriate revision marks to indicate your corrections. Circle any changes you make.
References: Consult the appropriate rules in Sections 1–4 as you complete this exercise.

On the other hand there are some New Yorkers, who think the   1
worst of their neighbors in the big apple. About eight-thirty   2
a.m.--I think it was June sixth--a lawyer named Paul Cronin was   3
standing inside a subway car, waiting for the train to pull out   4
of the station. Standing right next to him was a well-dressed,   5
professional-looking man. Just as the train was getting ready to   6
leave the well-dressed man bolted for the closing door bumping   7
into Paul in the process. Paul instinctively felt for his   8
wallet, and realized at once that it was not there. He ran after   9
the pickpocket and caught him by the lapel just as the door was   10
closing. In fact, when the door closed, Paul's hand was extended   11
outside the door and was still clutching the pickpocket's lapel.   12
As the train started to move, the horrified pickpocket had no   13
choice but to run alongside, because Paul was gripping his   14
lapel. Then the lapel came off the man's jacket.   15

Paul drew his hand back into the subway car, proudly   16
holding the lapel aloft. He didn't get his wallet back but he   17
had a trophy to show for his vigorous attempt to assert and   18
defend his rights. The passengers in the subway car all   19
applauded Paul for his brave efforts to stand up to a criminal.   20
Paul's colleagues at his law firm were equally admiring. Then   21
Paul's wife called.   22

"Darling, I don't want you to be worried," she said. "You   23
left your wallet on top of the dresser this morning".   24

9 Abbreviations

A. Directions: Provide the correct abbreviation, contraction, or short form for each of the following items. If an item is correct as given, write *C* in the answer column. **References:** ¶¶501–514. See Appendix D for the definition of any grammatical terms that you may not be familiar with.

1.	Mister	502b	11.	it is	505d
2.	Junior	502b	12.	Wednesday	506a
3.	Incorporated	502b	13.	miles per hour	507
4.	Part	502e	14.	Post Office	508
5.	continued	503	15.	United States of America	508
6.	kilobyte	503	16.	National Football League	508
7.	fiscal year	504	17.	doctor of philosophy	509
8.	department	505a	18.	limousine	510
9.	does not	505b	19.	District of Columbia	514
10.	let us	505b	20.	electronic mail	514

B. Directions: Circle any word or abbreviation that is incorrectly styled, and write the correct form in the answer column. If a sentence is correct as given, write *C* in the answer column. **References:** ¶¶501–514.

21.	Send the bill to the father—Roy Fox Senior—and not to his son.	21.	502b
22.	You have to read only Pt. One, not the complete book.	22.	502e
23.	Its about time that we decided whether to buy or lease a new car.	23.	505d
24.	Dr. Juanita Scott will represent us at the A.M.A. convention.	24.	508
25.	Last month Heather Dillingham moved to Washington, D.C..	25.	512

C. Directions: Provide the correct abbreviation or symbol for each of the following items. **References:** Consult the rules shown below as you complete this exercise.

26.	Ruth A. Goodman	516b	36.	February	532
27.	Esquire	518a	37.	Wednesday	532
28.	[John Dellums] the Third	518d	38.	inches	535a
29.	Certified Public Accountant	519g	39.	ounces	535a
30.	Internal Revenue Service	520a	40.	gram	537a 537a
31.	Corporation	520b	41.	kilometer	538a
32.	World Health Organization	524a	42.	chief executive officer	541
33.	Los Angeles	526	43.	shipping and handling	541
34.	North America	528a	44.	48 pounds	543
35.	Southeast	531	45.	World Wide Web	544a

Name _____ Date _____ Class _____ 25

D. Directions: Circle any word or abbreviation that is incorrectly styled, and write the correct form in the answer column. If a sentence is correct as given, write *C* in the answer column. **References:** Consult the rules shown below.

46.	Please schedule a meeting with E.G. Cavatelli.	46. _____	516a
47.	Doctor Chang is the best heart surgeon in the state.	47. _____	517a
48.	I wish Gov. Haas would state her position on the budget.	48. _____	517d
49.	Please refer this matter to my attorney, Mr. Eugene Dill, Esq.	49. _____	518c
50.	My primary physician is Dr. Nancy J. Wolfson, M.D.	50. _____	519c
51.	Have you seen the results of the latest C.N.N. poll?	51. _____	523
52.	He is campaigning throughout the U.S.	52. _____	525
53.	A friend of mine from Oberlin, Oh., just moved to Seattle.	53. _____	527b
54.	I usually fly to Ft. Lauderdale rather than to Miami.	54. _____	529
55.	Their new offices are located at 227 N. Fullerton Avenue.	55. _____	530b

E. Directions: Rewrite the following sentences to correct any errors in abbreviation style. **References:** Consult the rules shown below as you complete this exercise.

56. Dr. Marie Gallagher, Ph. D., has been named C.E.O. of Parametrics, Incorp. _____
_____

519c
519a
541
520b

57. Whenever I try to get cash from an A.T.M. machine, I always forget my P.I.N. number. _____
_____

508
522a
522e

58. Doctor P.J. Malone has been elected to the board of the N.A.A.C.P. _____
_____

517a
516a
508

59. According to Ms Sokolov's memo., the meeting scheduled for 3 PM on the 2nd of June has been

canceled. _____
_____

517a
533
510
503

60. Prof. Jon Lund II. is moving to Saint Petersburg after his retirement._____
_____

517d
518d
529b

F. Directions: Edit the following paragraph to correct any errors in abbreviations and contractions. Use appropriate proofreaders' marks (shown on pages 358–359 and on the inside back cover of *The Gregg Reference Manual*) to indicate your corrections. Circle any changes you make. **References:** Consult the appropriate rules in Section 5 as you complete this exercise.

```
If you want to participate in the experimental drug study now being            1
undertaken by the National Institute of Mental Health, I suggest you ask your   2
doctor to write to Dr. R.G. Valdez, M.D., who is setting up research sites      3
throughout the U.S.  The N.I.M.H. is based in Rockville, Maryland, but Doctor   4
Valdez works out of a lab in Washington, D. C.  Prof. George Y. Petrus Junior,  5
who lives here in town, knows Dr. Valdez personally, so he may be able to put   6
you in touch with her.  I don't have his phone number, but his office is        7
located at 212 E. Mountain Avenue.                                             8
```

10 Plurals

A. Directions: In the answer column, provide the correct plural form for each of the following items. **References:** Consult the rules shown below as you complete this exercise. See Appendix D for the definition of any grammatical terms that you may not be familiar with.

1. idea	601		11. thief	608b	
2. business	602		12. woman	609	
3. search	602		13. child	610	
4. fax	602		14. photocopy	611	
5. policy	604		15. sister-in-law	612a	
6. attorney	605		16. hang-up	612b	
7. stereo	606		17. finder's fee	612d	
8. weirdo	607a		18. alumnus	614	
9. potato	607b		19. criterion	614	
10. belief	608a		20. crisis	614	

B. Directions: Circle any word that is misspelled or misused, and write the correct form in the answer column. If a sentence is correct as given, write *C* in the answer column. **References:** Consult the rules shown below.

21. We can't base important decisions on Larry Cresskill's hunchs.   21. _____ 602

22. How many copys do you want us to distribute?   22. _____ 604

23. I'll get back to you as soon as I've heard from my attornies.   23. _____ 605

24. My two brother-in-laws think they have the answer to every problem.   24. _____ 612a

25. Getting the job done right is the only criteria we need to meet.   25. _____ 614

C. Directions: In the answer column, provide the correct plural form for each of the following items. **References:** Consult the rules shown below.

26. menu	601		36. Mr. and Mrs. Rossi	the	615a
27. crash	602		37. Mr. and Mrs. Jones	the	615b
28. company	604		38. Mr. and Mrs. Marx	the	615b
29. journey	605		39. Mr. and Mrs. Kenny	the	615c
30. memo	607a		40. No.		619
31. hero	607b		41. ft		620a
32. shelf	608b		42. p. (for *page*)		621a
33. rule of thumb	612a		43. M.D.		622a
34. phenomenon	614		44. 1990	the	624a
35. analysis	614		45. do and don't		625a

Name _____ Date _____ Class _____   27

D. Directions: Circle any word that is misspelled or misused, and write the correct form in the answer column. If a sentence is correct as given, write *C* in the answer column. **References:** Consult the rules shown below as you complete this exercise.

46. I have received job offers from three agencys.   46. _____ 604

47. We have no one to blame but ourselfs.   47. _____ 608b

48. Paul St. Germain is an alumni of Johns Hopkins University.   48. _____ 614

49. Yesterday's solar eclipse is one phenomena I will never forget.   49. _____ 614

50. Have you done an analyses of our sales for the first half of the year?   50. _____ 614

51. We have managed to get through worse crisises in the past.   51. _____ 614

52. We invited Mr. and Mrs. Murphy, but the Murphies were away.   52. _____ 615c

53. How many Ph.D.'s do we have in our Research Department?   53. _____ 622a

54. Our business grew tremendously during the 90s.   54. _____ 624a

55. I can't stand the weather when the temperature climbs into the 90s.   55. _____ 624a

E. Directions: Rewrite the following sentences to correct any errors in plural forms. **References:** Consult the rules shown below as you complete this exercise.

56. My bookshelfs are crammed with studys analyzing different types of taxs. _____ 611
_____ 604
                                                                  602

57. Please correct all the typoes in this memo, and change all the dashs to parenthesis. _____ 607a
_____ 602
                                                                  614

58. (For a list of the runner-ups, see p. 26-28.) _____
_____ 612a
                                                                  621a

59. Two of our committees have gone to great lengthes to review the pro's and con's of your plan. ___ 601
_____ 625a

60. My son has five parking summons and ten alibies for not paying them. _____ 602
_____ 601

F. Directions: Edit the following paragraph to correct any errors in plural forms. Use appropriate proofreaders' marks (shown on pages 358–359 and on the inside back cover of *The Gregg Reference Manual*) to indicate your corrections. Circle any changes you make. **References:** Consult the appropriate rules in ¶¶601–626 as you complete this exercise.

```
    The head of our HMO is planning a reception for the three new M.D.'s and      1

their wifes--the Jones, the McCarthies, and the Hastings. If the temperature     2

does not drop into the '70s, the reception will be held outdoors at the home     3

of Mr. and Mrs. Harvey Fox. The Foxs are going all out to make this a special    4

occasion. (No one could ever accuse them of being couch potatos.) They are       5

considering different menues and making arrangements for musical entertain-      6

ment. Many VIP will be invited. There is only one criteria for this event--      7

to do whatever is necessary to make the newcomers feel welcome.                  8
```

28

Copyright © 2005 by the McGraw-Hill Companies, Inc. All rights reserved.

11 Possessives

A. Directions: For each singular noun in the first column, provide the correct form for the singular possessive, the plural, and the plural possessive. **References:** Consult the rules shown below as you complete this exercise. See Appendix D for the definition of any grammatical terms that you may not be familiar with.

SINGULAR	SINGULAR POSSESSIVE	PLURAL	PLURAL POSSESSIVE
1. company	630a	604	632a
2. attorney	630a	605	632a
3. hero	630a	607b	632a
4. alumna (f.)	630a	614	633
5. Mr. and Mrs. Bono	630a	the 615a	the 632a
6. woman	630a	609	633
7. child	630a	610	633
8. Mr. French	630a	the 615b	the 632a
9. actress	631a	602	632a
10. Mr. Van Ness	631a	the 615b	the 632a
11. homeowner	634	611	635a
12. vice president	634	612a	635a
13. daughter-in-law	634	612a	635b
14. CPA	638	622a	638
15. M.D.	638	622a	638

B. Directions: Circle all errors in possessive forms in each of the following sentences, and write the correct form in the answer column. If a sentence is correct as given, write *C* in the answer column. **References:** ¶¶627–633.

16. My husband and I are going on a two weeks cruise to Alaska.　　16. _____ 627 629 632a

17. I'm opening a saving's account for my new granddaughter.　　17. _____ 628a 628a

18. Would you be willing to raise funds for the boys hockey team?　　18. _____ 632a 629

19. When we went to Mr. and Mrs. Smith's house, we met the Smith's sons.　　19. _____ 632a

20. I'm moving to Iowa. What do you know about Des Moines's schools?　　20. _____ 630b

21. Before you apply for a leave, you will need to get your boss' okay.　　21. _____ 631a

22. We take real pride in Massachusetts' historical struggle for freedom.　　22. _____ 631b 631b

23. Have you ever walked through New Orlean's French Quarter?　　23. _____ 631c

24. Burke & Feldman is having a sale on womens' and children's clothing.　　24. _____ 633 635a

25. The two eyewitness's statements don't agree on many key points.　　25. _____ 632b

Name _____ Date _____ Class _____

C. Directions: Rewrite the following sentences to eliminate all errors in possessive forms and awkward expressions.
References: Consult the rules shown below as you complete this exercise.

26. My sons-in-law's business will require me providing a lot of financial support. _____ 635b
_____ 647a

27. If this wallet is not her's, who's is it? _____
_____ 636

28. I got a great price on these Levis at Blue Genius Inc.s end-of-winter sale. _____ 640a
644
_____ 639

29. Do you think Frank's and Arnold's partnership will last? They don't respect each others' views.
643a
_____ 637

30. The organizers of our local farmer's market think this year's sales are twice as good as last

year. _____
652
_____ 644

31. We've been invited to a New Years' Eve party at the Russos. _____
650a
_____ 644

32. I asked for fast delivery of several hundred dollars worth of kitchen equipment, but the ship-

ment is now three week's overdue. _____
_____ 646
647a

33. What did your boss think about you asking for two week's vacation during the August sale? 627
629
_____ 632a

34. One of my author's manuscript has been accepted by a publisher, but I don't like the contract's

terms. _____
648c
_____ 645

35. Did you read Ms. Fox, the producer's comments about our doctor's son's acting career?_____
641
_____ 649

D. Directions: Edit the following paragraph to correct any errors in possessive forms. Use appropriate proofreaders' marks (shown on pages 358–359 and on the inside back cover of *The Gregg Reference Manual*) to indicate your corrections. Circle any changes you make. **References:** Consult the appropriate rules in ¶¶627–652 as you complete this exercise.

```
      Do you remember me telling you about Pam's and Marsha's shop going out of      1

business? They had a fantastic sale last week on womens clothes. This year's        2

prices were even lower than last year. I found a new dress for the Rossi's          3

anniversary celebration next month. (I like it very much, but I don't think         4

it's as nice as your's.) Then I remembered wanting new clothes for the one          5

weeks' trip to Orlando this spring. The shop had a wonderful price on Levis,        6

so I scooped up three pairs. Before I knew it, I had bought several hundred         7

dollars worth of clothes I probably don't need. I'm going to have to dip deep       8

into my saving's account to pay for this wild shopping spree. I hope there is       9

something left to pay for the trip to Orlando.                                     10
```

12 Spelling

A. Directions: Combine the base word with the suffix for each of the following items, and provide the correct spelling in the answer column. **References:** ¶¶701–709. See Appendix D for the definition of any grammatical terms that you may not be familiar with.

1.	ship + ing	_____ 701	11.	cheer + ful	_____ 705
2.	mad + en	_____ 701	12.	equip + ment	_____ 705
3.	control + ing	_____ 702	13.	trust + worthy	_____ 706
4.	occur + ed	_____ 702	14.	move + able	_____ 707a
5.	prefer + ence	_____ 702	15.	mile + age	_____ 707a
6.	ship + ment	_____ 703	16.	ice + y	_____ 707b
7.	mad + ness	_____ 703	17.	manage + able	_____ 707c
8.	cancel + ing	_____ 704	18.	like + ly	_____ 708
9.	total + ed	_____ 704	19.	nine + th	_____ 708
10.	program + ing	_____ 704	20.	lie + ing	_____ 709

B. Directions: Circle all spelling errors and write the correct forms in the answer column. If a sentence is correct as given, write *C* in the answer column. **References:** ¶¶701–709.

21. The number of students cutting classes is begining to decrease.　　21. _____ 701 702

22. Swimming at the beach is forbiden when lifeguards are not present.　　22. _____ 701 702 703

23. The shipment of relief supplies was cancelled without any explanation.　　23. _____ 704 702

24. The uncloging of traffic on Route 101 has benefited all commuters.　　24. _____ 704 702

25. Eyewitnesses differed in their accounts of how the accident occurred.　　25. _____ 704 704

26. Has anyone profited from the biassed reporting about the election?　　26. _____ 705

27. Todd and Jeff are argueing about whose car gets better mileage.　　27. _____ 707a 707b

28. Finding knowledgeable workers in this field is not easey.　　28. _____ 707c

29. Good management requires excellent judgment.　　29. _____ 708 707a

30. I said that Eve was dyeing her shoes; I did not say that she was dieing.　　30. _____ 709

C. Directions: If any of the following words are misspelled, write the correct spellings in the answer column. If a word is correct as given, write *C* in the answer column. **References:** Consult the rules shown below.

31.	worryed	_____ 710a	36.	weird	_____ 712
32.	shyly	_____ 710a	37.	recieve	_____ 712
33.	delayed	_____ 711	38.	thier	_____ 712
34.	sayed	_____ 711	39.	probible	_____ 713a
35.	beleif	_____ 712	40.	possable	_____ 713b

Name _____ Date _____ Class _____　　31

41.	persistant	_____	714	46.	advertize	_____	715b
42.	resistant	_____	714	47.	analise	_____	715c
43.	assistence	_____	714	48.	supercede	_____	716a
44.	relevance	_____	714	49.	procede	_____	716b
45.	realise	_____	715a	50.	precede	_____	716c

D. Directions: Circle all spelling errors and write the correct forms in the answer column. If a sentence is correct as given, write *C* in the answer column. **References:** Consult the rules shown below as you complete this exercise.

51.	What is the likelyhood that this fad will spread countrywide?	51. _____	710a
52.	I don't have a weight problem; I have a hieght problem.	52. _____	712
53.	Do you think the defendent's testimony is credible?	53. _____	713b 714
54.	They do a better job of advertising thier merchandise than we do.	54. _____	712 715
55.	You will have to concede that the existing proceedure is not working.	55. _____	716b–c

E. Directions: If the boldface word in each of the following items is misspelled, write the correct form in the answer column. If the item is correct as given, write *C* in the answer column. **References:** ¶720.

56.	happy to **accomodate** you	_____	66.	plan an **itinery**	_____
57.	to make your **aquaintance**	_____	67.	serve as the **liason**	_____
58.	is **basicly** all right	_____	68.	a **momento** of the occasion	_____
59.	need to check the **calender**	_____	69.	that's your **privaledge**	_____
60.	falls in the second **catagory**	_____	70.	order a large **quanity**	_____
61.	to achieve a **concensus**	_____	71.	maintain **seperate** accounts	_____
62.	wants a **definate** answer	_____	72.	find something **similiar**	_____
63.	**elimanate** the frills	_____	73.	need to regain your **strenth**	_____
64.	on the 14th of **Febuary**	_____	74.	a drop in the **temperture**	_____
65.	reach his full **heighth**	_____	75.	meet every **Wensday**	_____

F. Directions: Edit the following paragraph to correct any spelling errors. Use appropriate proofreaders' marks (shown on pages 358–359 and on the inside back cover of *The Gregg Reference Manual*) to indicate your corrections. Circle any changes you make. **References:** Consult the appropriate rules in Section 7 as you complete this exercise.

```
      Whenever my wife and I discuss vacation arrangements, we often conclude        1

that we should plan seperate itineries. Basicly, the problem is this: she          2

likes cold weather and I become miserable when the temperture drops into the       3

30s. I have tried to accomodate her preferrences, but we start argueing            4

nevertheless. Last year we agreed on a trip and then cancelled it at the last      5

minute. I keep thinking that it should be possible to find a vacation spot         6

that will satisfy both of us, but I realise that it's not going to be easy.        7
```

32

13 Choosing the Right Word

A. Directions: If the boldface word in each of the following items is misspelled or misused, write the correct form in the answer column. If an item is correct as given, write *C* in the answer column. **References:** ¶719.

1. denied **excess** to the files _____
2. looking for good **advise** _____
3. worked as a health **aid** _____
4. found **alot** of errors _____
5. your **assistants** was helpful _____
6. more pressure than I can **bare** _____
7. step on the **breaks** _____
8. take a deep **breathe** _____
9. that **can not** be true _____
10. to **cease** the opportunity _____
11. choose a **cite** for the new office _____
12. a member of the town **counsel** _____
13. make daily entries in a **dairy** _____
14. will not tolerate any **descent** _____
15. to **differ** a decision for a week _____

16. to **disperse** company funds _____
17. ten **discreet** groups of voters _____
18. need a **disinterested** observer _____
19. damage **dew** to moisture _____
20. to **illicit** many opinions _____
21. an **imminent** politician _____
22. an unsealed **envelop** _____
23. was not **phased** by the insult _____
24. a very courageous **feet** _____
25. displayed a **flare** for writing _____
26. to **flout** one's possessions _____
27. to **forego** my right to protest _____
28. I **formally** taught math _____
29. went **fourth** to help others _____
30. their stories do not **gibe** _____

B. Directions: If the boldface word in each of the following items is misspelled or misused, write the correct form in the answer column. If an item is correct as given, write *C* in the answer column. **References:** ¶719.

31. eat more **healthy** foods _____
32. had not **herd** the news reports _____
33. it's **holy** understandable _____
34. marched down the **isle** _____
35. to be **libel** for the damage _____
36. to be afraid of **lightening** _____
37. I'm **loathe** to take on that job _____
38. Sue **maybe** the one we hire _____
39. a **miner** irritation _____
40. these bills are **overdo** _____
41. a lot of time has **past** _____
42. at the **peek** of his career _____
43. need to resist **pier** pressure _____
44. get at the **plane** truth _____
45. conduct a **pole** of local voters _____

46. to **pour** over the printouts _____
47. make one's **presents** felt _____
48. my **principle** goal in life _____
49. is **quiet** happy with her job _____
50. a starring **roll** in the play _____
51. to find the best **root** to Denver _____
52. to make a **seen** in public _____
53. uses expensive **stationary** _____
54. takes a different **tact** _____
55. the ropes must be **taught** _____
56. make a **through** search _____
57. worked much **to** hard _____
58. applied **undo** pressure _____
59. to **wave** your rights _____
60. to protect **you're** property _____

Name _____ Date _____ Class _____ 33

C. Directions: Select the correct form in parentheses for each of the following sentences, and write your answer in the answer column. **References:** ¶719.

61. Should we (accede, exceed) to Pamela Butler's request for a transfer?

61. _____

62. If you don't like my idea, do you have an (alternate, alternative) to offer?

62. _____

63. To whom should these purchases be (billed, build)?

63. _____

64. Helena is the (capital, capitol, Capitol) of Montana.

64. _____

65. We have ordered a five-(coarse, course) meal for Ms. Noriega's banquet.

65. _____

66. I can no longer cope with Mr. Whitman's (continual, continuous) complaints.

66. _____

67. We need to (device, devise) a fallback plan in case this plan doesn't work.

67. _____

68. This problem needs to be referred to a (higher, hire) level of management.

68. _____

69. Pretending not to understand was very (ingenious, ingenuous) on Carl's part.

69. _____

70. Under the circumstances it was the (leased, least) that we could do.

70. _____

71. At this point what do we have to (loose, lose)?

71. _____

72. It's not a good idea to (medal, meddle) in Christopher's affairs.

72. _____

73. Because of the heavy fog we (missed, mist) the turnoff to the lake.

73. _____

74. A doctor with a good bedside manner exhibits a lot of (patience, patients).

74. _____

75. There is a (perspective, prospective) buyer for our house.

75. _____

76. What is the best way for us to (precede, proceed)?

76. _____

77. Harry's requests must take (precedence, precedents) over everyone else's.

77. _____

78. The predictions of (profits, prophets) are often disregarded by their contemporaries.

78. _____

79. The Friday afternoon meetings are always a (waist, waste) of time.

79. _____

80. Eating two boxes of cookies at one sitting is not a good (way, weigh) to diet.

80. _____

D. Directions: Edit the following paragraph to correct any errors in spelling and usage. Use appropriate proofreaders' marks (shown on pages 358–359 and on the inside back cover of *The Gregg Reference Manual*) to indicate your corrections. Circle any changes you make. **References:** ¶719.

```
    If my friend Tom could be more discrete and use more tack in his dealings    1
with people, he would be more popular with his colleagues at work. I've tried    2
to give him alot of advise along these lines, but Tom says that he can not       3
bare to listen to me any longer. I think he's lost patience with me, and I'm     4
sure that he is reluctant to get some perspective on the way he appears to       5
other people. It maybe true that I have come on to strong in the past.           6
However, I believe that Tom is loathe to change his behavior. In fact, I         7
suspect that he is actually quiet satisfied with things as they are.             8
```

34

14 Compound Words

A. Directions: If a boldface item in the following list should be written as a solid word, insert the "delete space" mark (for example, by law). If a boldface item should be hyphenated, use the "insert hyphen" mark (for example, mixup). If a boldface item should be written as separate words, use the "insert space" mark (for example, crackdown). Circle any changes you make. If an item is correct as given, write *C* in the answer column. **References:** ¶¶801–808.

1. in a spirit of **good will**	801a	
2. need to use some **good sense**	801a	
3. time to say **good bye**	801a	
4. cut down on the **paper work**	801a	
5. who invented the **paper clip**	801a	
6. to **follow up** on his progress	802	
7. do a **follow up** on his memo	802	
8. we need to get a **go ahead**	802	
9. can we now **go ahead**	802	
10. cannot **makeup** their minds	802 803a	

11. when negotiations **breakdown**	802 803b
12. need to **check in** by 6 o'clock	802 803c
13. and watch sales **takeoff**	802 803f
14. to **takeover** the company	802 803g
15. engaged in a **free for all**	804a
16. get down to the **nitty gritty**	804b
17. ask the **editor in chief**	804c
18. good at **problem solving**	805a
19. had to go for an **Xray**	807
20. write to a **vice president**	808c

B. Directions: If any of the following expressions are considered unacceptable, write an appropriate alternative in the answer column. If an expression is acceptable, write *C* in the answer column. **References:** Consult the rules shown below as you complete this exercise.

21. layman	809a	
22. salesmen	809a	
23. mankind	809a	
24. workmen's comp	809a	
25. workmanship	809c	

26. Chairman Paul Foy	809d
27. woman doctor	810
28. stewardess	840a
29. authoress	840a
30. heroine	840a

C. Directions: Edit the boldface element in each of the following items to correct any misspellings. Use appropriate revision marks to indicate your corrections. Circle any changes you make. If an item is correct as given, write *C* in the answer column. **References:** ¶811–812.

31. to **high light** the key points	811a	
32. to **baby sit** for a neighbor	811a	
33. to **short change** a customer	811a	
34. to **spot check** the answers	811a	
35. **spot checking** the price list	812a	

36. to **double space** the report	811a
37. to leave a **double space**	812a
38. an **air conditioned** house	812a
39. **air conditioning** is essential	812a
40. **air conditioning** my bedroom	812a

Name _____ Date _____ Class _____

D. Directions: Edit the boldface element in each of the following sentences to correct any misspellings. Use appropriate proofreaders' marks to indicate your corrections. Circle any changes you make. If a sentence is correct as given, write *C* in the answer column. **References:** Consult the rules shown below as you complete this exercise.

41. A **well known** consultant will be helping us develop our **long range** plans. 41. _____ 813 / 814

42. I know that this is **high tech** equipment, but is it really **up to date**? 42. _____ 814 / 813

43. Everything said at this **high level** conference is **off the record**. 43. _____ 815a

44. Even though these goods are **high priced**, they are **tax exempt**. 44. _____ 815b

45. I'm enrolled in an **all day** program, so I can work only **part time**. 45. _____ 816a

46. I'm getting hit with a **7.5 percent** increase on my **$400 a month** apartment. 46. _____ 817a

47. I've requested a **three month** extension for the filing of my **income tax** return. 47. _____ 817a / 818a

48. Jack Egan is now an important **real estate** agent with **Park Avenue** clients. 48. _____ 818a / 819a

49. Pam runs a **mail order** business targeted at **African American** women. 49. _____ 818a / 818d

50. Phone us **toll free** if you want to take advantage of our **store wide** sale. 50. _____ 820a / 820c

51. This raincoat is not really **water proof** but it is **water repellent**. 51. _____ 820c / 820a

52. The level of our **health care related** costs is truly **mind boggling**. 52. _____ 821b / 821a

53. Under a **long standing** agreement, they send us the **best qualified** people. 53. _____ 822a / 822b

54. Your dog may be **friendly looking,** but his effect on me was **hair raising**. 54. _____ 822a / 821a

55. No one would ever accuse our **long winded** speaker of being **close mouthed**. 55. _____ 823a / 823c

56. The next speaker is **well known** for his **highly focused** presentations. 56. _____ 824b / 824a

57. Her speech was a **very trying** experience, because it lacked a **clear cut** focus. 57. _____ 825a / 824b

58. Perhaps their demands will be **scaled down** during this **cooling off** period. 58. _____ 826

59. We get **red hot** results by using **tried and true** techniques. 59. _____ 827d / 827b

60. I like Bob's **can do** spirit, but I'm taking a **wait and see** approach. 60. _____ 828a

61. I just got a **get well** card from my **ten year old** nephew. 61. _____ 829a / 831a

62. This **up to date** procedure is actually more **time consuming** than the old one. 62. _____ 831a / 821d

63. Fill out a **change of address** form if this information is not **up to date**. 63. _____ 831a / 831b

64. A **trial and error** approach won't work; it's time for a **go/no go** decision. 64. _____ 831d / 832a

65. Use **8½ by 11 inch** paper, and type it **single or double spaced**. 65. _____ 812a

E. Directions: Edit the following paragraph to correct any errors with compound words. Use appropriate proofreaders' marks to indicate your corrections, and circle any changes you make. **References:** ¶¶801–832.

```
    I just heard about Sam Perez's accident. I'm glad you sent him out for        1
X rays. If you handle the medical paper work, I'll follow-up with the woman       2
doctor at our clinic. Sam's in for some high priced treatment, but I'm sure       3
his injury will be covered by workmen's comp. In the meantime, try to get a       4
part time replacement for Sam for at least a three to four week period. I         5
will send out a company wide memo telling the staff about Sam's accident and      6
asking them to start picking out get well cards.                                  7
```

36

15 Using the Hyphen in Compounds and Word Division

A. Directions: For each of the following items combine the elements to form a word, and write the properly spelled word in the answer column. Use hyphens as necessary. **References:** Consult the rules shown below as you complete this exercise. See Appendix D for the definition of any grammatical terms that you may not be familiar with.

1.	audio + visual	833a	11.	co + operate	835b
2.	multi + purpose	833a	12.	co + owner	835b
3.	non + discriminatory	833a	13.	re + elect	835a
4.	non + civil service	833c	14.	pre + eminent	835a
5.	mid + afternoon	833a	15.	self + evident	836a
6.	mid + thirties	833a 844	16.	self + less	836b
7.	mid + March	838 844	17.	three + fold	833a
8.	anti + theft	833a	18.	thirty + ish	833a
9.	anti + inflationary	834	19.	senator + elect	808b
10.	anti + American	838	20.	ex + husband	808b

B. Directions: Edit the boldface elements in each of the following sentences to correct any spelling errors. Use appropriate proofreaders' marks (shown on pages 358–359 and on the inside back cover of *The Gregg Reference Manual*) to indicate your corrections. Circle any changes you make. If a sentence is correct as given, write *C* in the answer column. **References:** Consult the rules shown below as you complete this exercise.

21. This is a specially designed **pre-test** for **pre-high-school** students. 21. ___ 833a 833c 833a

22. Everyone should bring an **extra warm** sweater for **him or herself**. 22. ___ 836c 836a 832d

23. Our clinic offers **self help** programs for **over and under weight** people. 23. ___ 833 837

24. We can't decide whether to **release** our apartment or buy a **coop**. 24. ___ 835b 837

25. Please **resign** the contracts and return them in the **self addressed** envelope. 25. ___ 836a

C. Directions: In each of the following items the diagonal indicates where the item has been divided at the end of a line. In the answer column provide the number of the rule that explains why each word or phrase *should not* be divided in this way. **References:** ¶¶901–906 for items 26–35; ¶¶907–918 for items 36–45; ¶¶919–922 for items 46–55.

26.	ship-/ ped	36.	85,-/ 000	46.	pas-/ sing
27.	stra-/ ight	37.	self-as-/ surance	47.	beginn-/ ing
28.	AM-/ VETS	38.	hidea-/ way	48.	mill-/ ion
29.	are-/ n't	39.	oper-/ ator	49.	Mrs./ Sanchez
30.	a-/ cross	40.	radia-/ tor	50.	May/ 21, 2007
31.	tho-/ ugh	41.	su-/ pernatural	51.	page/ 42
32.	chew-/ y	42.	responsi-/ ble	52.	Ellen/ T. Mann
33.	let-/ up	43.	hope-/ lessness	53.	415/ Grove Street
34.	pres-/ sed	44.	undercur-/ rent	54.	three people/—Jay,
35.	stere-/ o	45.	read-/ dress	55.	as follows: (1)/ the

Name ___ Date ___ Class ___ 37

D. Directions: Rewrite the following sentences to correct all spelling errors and to remove all sexist expressions. **References:** Consult the rules shown below as you complete this exercise.

56. Please send an inter-office memo to all the salesmen, setting the date when they'll be asked to run-through their sales presentations. _____

     _____ 833a
     _____ 809a
                                      802

57. The woman lawyer who is representing my father in law has asked him to pin-point any discrepancies in the statements of the eye witnesses. _____

     _____ 810
     _____ 804c
     _____ 811a
                                      801a

58. Marilyn is the co-author of a number of 60 to 90 hour self study courses designed for businessmen who want to expand their operations._____

     _____ 835b
     _____ 832b
     _____ 836a
                                      809a

59. Please follow-up on the progress made by the newly-hired employees who recently completed our on the job training program. _____

     _____ 802
     _____ 824a
                                      831a

60. Please ask Ms. Washington to turnover all of the up to date production reports to George Gangi, our new vice-president. _____

     _____ 802
     _____ 831a
                                      808c

E. Directions: Edit the following paragraph to correct any errors involving compound words and division of word groups. Use appropriate proofreaders' marks to indicate your corrections, and circle any changes you make. **References:** Consult the appropriate rules in Sections 8 and 9 as you complete this exercise.

```
    Janice Darden and I are coowners of a small publishing company that        1
specializes in self help books for people like you and me--in other words,     2
the typical layman. We'd like to sign up a well known authoress named Fay      3
V. Fox. She's writing a book that tells people how to prepare their own        4
income tax returns and avoid the annual attack of mid April blues. Janice      5
thinks we'll have no trouble getting a go-ahead from Gloria's agent, but       6
I feel she's being overconfident. The agent has sent us a list of demands      7
--many of which we can't agree to. When we meet with the agent on October      8
23, I'm afraid our contract negotiations will quickly breakdown.               9
```

38

16 Editing Survey B

A. Directions: Rewrite the following sentences to correct all errors relating to abbreviations, plurals, possessives, spelling, and compound words. **References:** Consult the appropriate rules in Sections 5–8 as you complete this exercise.

1. Pt. Two (p. 94-162) analises the long term consequences of the environmental legislation past by Congress last year.

   _____

   _____

   _____

2. We are having a store wide sale during the month of Febuary in all of our branchs across the U.S.— with special discounts on womens' clothing.

   _____

   _____

   _____

3. Please enclose a self addressed envelop if you would like to recieve copys of Dr. Ross' speeches at this years' AMA convention.

   _____

   _____

   _____

4. The temperture in Washington, D. C., last winter never went below the '30s, according to our real-estate agent, Mrs. Galsworthy's letter.

   _____

   _____

   _____

5. P.V. Hunsinger is well-known for her analysises of various poles designed to measure consumer's confidence in the economy.

   _____

   _____

   _____

6. The company's attornies have advised our C.E.O. to take a wait and see attitude until the Supreme Court hands down it's judgement in the Sampson case.

_____

_____

_____

7. On the basis of faxs from our salesmen in the field, this year's orders for our line of stationary products are not likely to excede last year.

_____

_____

_____

8. From a long range prospective there maybe to many PhD's graduating over the next ten years and not alot of job opportunitys opening up for them.

_____

_____

_____

9. Please set-up an all day meeting to discuss ways to elemenate several million dollars worth of expenses incurred by our agencys in Chicago and Saint Louis.

_____

_____

_____

10. There is only one clear cut criteria for success in this business: how well you accomodate your customer's preferrences, no matter what they maybe.

_____

_____

_____

40

Editing Survey B (Continued)

B. Directions: Edit the following paragraphs to correct all errors. Use appropriate proofreaders' marks (shown on pages 358–359 and on the inside back cover of *The Gregg Reference Manual*) to indicate your corrections. Circle any changes you make. **References:** Consult the appropriate rules in Sections 1–8 as you complete this exercise.

```
     I don't have answers to all the problems that one faces but       1
I can tell you about a technique that can get you through some          2
of life's difficult moments. I learned this technique from a            3
brief anecdote that appeared in the "Reader's Digest" a number          4
of years ago.                                                           5
     A woman, who was traveling to see her grandchildren, found         6
herself stranded at O'Hare Airport in Chicago because of bad            7
weather. All flights had been cancelled since mid-afternoon,            8
and 100's of unhappy travelers were waiting all over the Air-           9
port. Every seat had been taken. Travelers were now sitting            10
and lying on the floor, all suffering that terrible frustration        11
that comes from not being able to control one's situation.             12
Nearby was a young mother with a five-year-old child squirming         13
in her lap, whining and whimpering and being altogether impos-         14
sible. The mother was a model of saintly patience. She simply          15
crooned, "There, there, Nancy. It's going to be all right. In a        16
little while you'll be home. You'll have a nice bath and then           17
put on a fresh nightgown and slip into bed for a good nights'           18
sleep." Over and over she crooned, "There, there, Nancy."              19
     About 7 PM the weather started to clear. The grandmother          20
heard the boarding announcement for her plane. As she was about        21
to leave the area she felt the impulse to speak to the young           22
mother. "I want to tell you," she said, "that I think you are          23
the most wonderful mother I have ever seen. Your patience is           24
remarkable. I love the way you talk to your daughter Nancy."           25
     The mother looked up with surprise. "Oh," she said, "her          26
name is Emily. My name is Nancy."                                      27
                                                                       28
```

C. Directions: Edit the following paragraphs to correct all errors. Use appropriate proofreaders' marks to indicate your corrections. Circle any changes you make. **References:** Consult the appropriate rules in Sections 1–9 as you complete this exercise.

According to one disgruntled author, editors winnow out the   1
wheat from the chaff, and publish the chaff. Perhaps the reason   2
that editors are so often disliked is that they so often speak with   3
a sharp tongue. Doctor Samuel Johnson, the great 18th century   4
author and critic, offered this comment on a writer's manuscript: 5
"What you have written is both good and original. Unfortunately,   6
the parts that are good are not original, and the parts that are   7
original are not good." Charles Dickens also possessed a sharp   8
tongue. After reviewing an unpublished collection of poems en-   9
titled "Orient Pearls at Random Strung," he gave the following   10
verdict: "Too much string."   11

Is it possible that some children are destined to become   12
editors from an early age. It certainly seems that way with   13
our's. When our son Christopher was four, he announced that   14
Alpha-Bits was his favorite cereal. He said that he liked it   15
because the cereal was "made out of letters." Kate, his six   16
year old sister, corrected him. "No, Chris," she said, "it's   17
the cereal that's made *into* letters." He punched her, re-   18
vealing that the instinct to strike back at one's editor starts   19
early.   20

The editorial tradition in our family seems to be con-   21
tinuing into the next generation. Our son John was preparing   22
breakfast for his three-year-old daughter. As he started to   23
spread jam on her toast, he realized that she wanted to be-   24
come more directly involved in the process. He said, "do   25
you want to put the jam on yourself?" "No, Daddy," she re-   26
plied. "I want to put it on the toast."   27

I'm afraid that you can not change editors, that's just the   28
way they are.   29

17 Grammar: Subjects and Verbs

A. Directions: First review how the principal parts of regular and irregular verbs are formed (see ¶1030 and ¶1035). Then, for each boldface verb in the following sentences, write the specified tense of the verb in the answer column. **References:** Consult the rules shown below as you complete the exercise. See Appendix D for the definition of any grammatical terms that you may not be familiar with.

1. **Present tense:** Alan always **do** an excellent job of summarizing our discussions.

1. _____ 1031b 1035b

2. **Future tense:** Natalie **finish** the statistical analysis that you started.

2. _____ 1031c

3. **Past tense:** Mr. Porter **go** to Chicago last week to meet with his lawyers.

3. _____ 1032a 1030b

4. **Present perfect tense:** I **have see** the review of your new book on telecommunications.

4. _____ 1033a 1030b

5. **Present progressive tense:** We **are issue** new directives to our staff this week.

5. _____ 1034a 1030a

6. **Past progressive tense:** Jan **was cancel** her credit cards all during the week.

6. _____ 1034b 1030a

7. **Present perfect progressive tense:** Our sales **have been slip** continually.

7. _____ 1034d 1030a 1036

8. **Present passive tense:** I **am expect** to do the work of two people.

8. _____ 1036 1030a

9. **Past passive tense:** Charlie **was choose** to head the Eastern Region's sales staff.

9. _____ 1036 1030b

10. **Present perfect passive tense:** They **have been transfer** to the Boston office.

10. _____ 1036 1030a

B. Directions: If any of the boldface verbs are incorrectly used in the following sentences, write the correct form in the answer column. If a sentence is correct as given, write *C* in the answer column. **References:** ¶¶1030–1033.

11. **Past tense:** I liked the movie *Burnt by the Sun* so much that I **seen** it four times.

11. _____ 1032b 1030b

12. **Past tense:** Christopher **done** the whole report without any help from others on staff.

12. _____ 1032b 1030b

13. **Past tense:** Timothy **brung** me the news about your graduating with honors.

13. _____ 1032b

14. **Past tense:** We **begun** the board meeting without waiting for Mrs. Farragut.

14. _____ 1032b

Name _____ Date _____ Class _____   43

15. **Past tense:** This sweatshirt **shrank** about two sizes after only one washing.

15. _____ 1032b

16. **Present perfect tense:** The temperature **has rose** to 90°F every day this week.

16. _____ 1033

17. **Present perfect tense:** My neighbor, John Forest, **has broke** my lawn mower for the last time.

17. _____ 1033

18. **Present perfect tense:** I **have wrote** only two job application letters so far this month.

18. _____ 1033 1030b

C. Directions: The subject of an independent or dependent clause appears in boldface in each of the following sentences. Select the correct verb form in parentheses, and write your answer in the answer column. **References:** Consult the rules shown below as you complete this exercise.

19. It is essential that these **orders** (are, be) shipped by the end of the week.

19. _____ 1038a

20. It is urgent that **Molly** (prepare, prepares) a revised draft of the report.

20. _____ 1038b

21. I wish **I** (was, were) more at ease during my weekly meetings with Mrs. Hennessey.

21. _____ 1039a

22. If **I** (was, were) better coordinated, I would take up cross-country skiing.

22. _____ 1040

23. If **I** (had, would have) been asked to speak, I would have gladly done so.

23. _____ 1040

24. Phil acts as if **he** (was, were) the greatest computer programmer in the world.

24. _____ 1042

25. Sarah said that **she** (is, was) planning to return to college this fall.

25. _____ 1047

D. Directions: The subject of an independent or dependent clause appears in boldface in each of the following sentences. Select the verb form in parentheses that agrees with the boldface subject, and write your answer in the answer column. **References:** Consult the rules shown below as you complete this exercise.

26. **I** (am, is) the only person who can manage to get along with clients like Mr. Henderson.

26. _____ 1001a

27. Only **you** (has, have) the full confidence of all the members of the board.

27. _____ 1001a

28. **Jennifer Waterman** (doesn't, don't) handle incoming calls as well as she should.

28. _____ 1001a

29. **We** (was, were) quite disappointed by the company's performance last year.

29. _____ 1001a

Grammar: Subjects and Verbs (Continued)

30. **They** (has, have) been devising a new organization for the entire company.

30. _____ 1001a

31. **Tom and Greg** (is, are) going to attend the conference in London with me.

31. _____ 1002a

32. Every **car, van, and truck** (is, are) on sale during the next two weeks.

32. _____ 1002c

33. **Either Helen or her mother** (has, have) walked off with the keys to my condo.

33. _____ 1003

34. **Neither Ms. Welling nor the Silbers** (is, are) planning to attend the reception.

34. _____ 1005

35. The **invoice** for these laptop computers (contains, contain) many errors.

35. _____ 1006a

36. The **CEO,** along with his top managers, (is, are) leaving for Tokyo tomorrow.

36. _____ 1006a 1007

37. **One** of the photocopiers (is, are) going to be taken out of service again.

37. _____ 1008a

38. Each **strategy** that you have proposed (has, have) to be carefully evaluated.

38. _____ 1009a

39. **Everybody** in the audience (seems, seem) enthusiastic about the performance.

39. _____ 1010

40. **Many** of us (was, were) not asked to provide our reactions to the new ad campaign.

40. _____ 1012

E. Directions: The subject of an independent or dependent clause appears in boldface in each of the following sentences. Select the correct verb form in parentheses, and write your answer in the answer column. **References:** Consult the rules shown below as you complete this exercise.

41. **All** of the proceeds from this campaign (is, are) being donated to the United Way.

41. _____ 1013a

42. **None** of the applicants (was, were) hired for this job opening. *(General usage)*

42. _____ 1013b

43. The **criteria** (has, have) been revised by the executive compensation committee.

43. _____ 1018a 614

44. The **jury** (has, have) finally agreed on a verdict.

44. _____ 1019a

45. **A number** of employees (has, have) signed up for the grammar seminar.

45. _____ 1023

Name _____ Date _____ Class _____ 45

46. **The number** of employees who signed up (was, were) not as large as I had hoped.

46. _____ 1023

47. **Two-thirds** of the community (supports, support) the plan to build a new high school.

47. _____ 1025a

48. **Two-thirds** of the voters (supports, support) the plan to build a new high school.

48. _____ 1025b

49. What actions (am, are) **I** supposed to take on the basis of Jim Farley's memo?

49. _____ 1027a

50. Before we can make a decision, there (is, are) many **factors** that need to be weighed.

50. _____ 1028a

F. Directions: Edit the following paragraph to correct any errors. Use appropriate proofreaders' marks (shown on pages 358–359 and on the inside back cover of *The Gregg Reference Manual*) to indicate your corrections. Circle any changes you make. **References:** Consult the appropriate rules in ¶¶1001–1047 as you complete this exercise.

```
    I wish I was a better athlete. Unfortunately, my body          1
don't respond extremely well to the directions issued by my        2
brain.  My problems started early. I crashed my tricycle into a    3
car, and my collarbone was broke as a result. I done the same      4
thing to my collarbone the following year. My roller skates        5
came apart as I begun to go down a slight incline. One of my       6
friends have reminded me of the time when I, along with some       7
classmates, were cutting through a gas station on a bicycle. On    8
that occasion I flew headfirst over the handlebars into an ele-    9
gant pyramid of oilcans. There is probably some extremely good    10
explanations for my lack of coordination, but none of those       11
explanations interests me. A number of my neighbors has tried     12
to get me to go jogging with them, but I always respond with the  13
words of Robert Maynard Hutchins: "Whenever I feel like exercise, 14
I lie down until the feeling passes."                             15
```

46

A. Directions: In the answer column write the correct pronouns for the boldface words in the following sentences. If a sentence is correct as given, write *C* in the answer column. **References:** Consult the rules shown below as you complete this exercise. See Appendix D for the definition of any grammatical terms that you may not be familiar with.

1. **Subject:** Betty and **me** can make all the necessary arrangements ourselves.

2. **Subject:** I thought that Bob and **her** did an especially nice job on the annual report.

3. **Subject:** The Boyles and **us** have theater tickets for this Saturday night.

4. **Subject:** The Pavlicks and **them** can't seem to agree on the terms of the contract.

5. **Direct object:** They have invited Mr. Worthington and **I** to the reception for the new CEO.

6. **Indirect object:** We sent the Rossis and **they** bouquets from our garden.

7. **Object of preposition:** This matter concerns no one except you and **I**.

8. **Subject of infinitive:** Jane asked Frank and **I** to keep her decision a secret.

9. **Possessive:** I thought that this copy of the long-range plan was **her's.**

10. **Possessive:** Did you think that this copy of the long-range plan was really **yours'?**

11. **Possessive:** The corporation was not very happy about **us** talking to the reporters.

12. **Possessive:** Our company would like **it's** employees to participate in the drive.

13. **Following** *than:* Mary Lee can speak Spanish much more fluently than **me.**

14. **Following** *as:* I have never been able to cope with these crises as well as **her.**

15. **Compound personal pronoun:** Cynthia and **myself** drafted the memo to Ms. Ruby.

1. _____ 1054a
2. _____ 1054a
3. _____ 1054a
4. _____ 1054a
5. _____ 1055a
6. _____ 1055a
7. _____ 1055b
8. _____ 1055c
9. _____ 1056c
10. _____ 1056c
11. _____ 1056d
12. _____ 1056e
13. _____ 1057
14. _____ 1057
15. _____ 1060

B. Directions: The antecedent of each pronoun appears in boldface in each of the following sentences. Select the correct pronoun forms in parentheses, and write your answers in the answer column. **References:** ¶¶1049, 1054–1056.

16. **Gloria** feels that (she, her) should be allowed to set (her, hers) own hours.

16. _____ 1049a
1054
1056b

17. **I** have (my, mine) own opinion of Tim's behavior, just as **you** have (your's, yours).

17. _____ 1049a
1056

18. **We** need to plan (our, our's) response when the **investigators** release (their, they're) report.

18. _____ 1049a
1056

19. **Rita and Fran** said (she, they) were eager to offer (her, their) services.

19. _____ 1049b
1054
1056

20. **Neither Rita nor Fran** said (she, they) wanted to offer (her, their) services.

20. _____ 1049c
1056

C. Directions: If any of the boldface words are incorrectly used in the following sentences, write the correct form in the answer column. If a sentence is correct as given, write *C* in the answer column. **References:** ¶1056e.

21. Do you think **its** a good idea to revise our schedule of prices and discounts?

21. _____

22. Every component of this computer has **it's** own design and manufacturing standards.

22. _____

23. Do you think that the company can afford to increase **its** dividend this year?

23. _____

24. After all, **its** your money and you can spend it in any way that you want.

24. _____

25. I heard that **your** moving to North Carolina later this year.

25. _____

26. Do you plan to sell **you're** house before you move?

26. _____

27. I think **your** off to a great start in developing a business plan.

27. _____

28. **Their** buying a larger house to accommodate their rapidly growing family.

28. _____

29. **Theirs** no use complaining about things that can't be fixed.

29. _____

30. My ideas on how to cut taxes and government spending are different from **their's**.

30. _____

48

Grammar: Pronouns (Continued)

D. Directions: First read ¶¶1050–1052 carefully. Then edit the following sentences, applying the technique suggested by the rule number in each case. Use appropriate proofreaders' marks (shown on pages 358–359 and on the inside back cover of *The Gregg Reference Manual*) to indicate your corrections. Circle any changes you make. **References:** ¶¶1050–1053, 1060.

31. Every good writer of fiction has his own distinctive way of portraying human experience.

    1052a

32. Every good writer of fiction has his own distinctive way of portraying human experience.

    1052b

33. Every parent wants his children to have access to the best schools and the best teachers.

    1053a
    1052b

34. Neither one of the ads created the additional sales that they were supposed to.

    1053a

35. If anyone does not understand this procedure, you should speak to myself at once.

    1053d
    1060

E. Directions: Each item below contains two sentences. The first sentence requires you to select the correct pronoun in parentheses and write your answer in the answer column. The second sentence—in parentheses—should help you make the correct selection in each case. **References:** ¶¶1061–1063.

36. (Who/Whom) did you say was waiting to see me? (You said **she** was waiting to see me.)

    36. _____ 1061c

37. Please give this package to (whoever/whomever) asks for it at the front desk. (**She** asks for it.)

    37. _____ 1061c

38. Mr. Fogel, (who/whom) you spoke to last week, has called again. (You spoke to **him** last week.)

    38. _____ 1061d

39. I need a financial planner (who/whom) I can rely on. (I can rely on **her.**)

    39. _____ 1061d

40. (Who/Whom) are you going to vote for? (You are going to vote for **him.**)

    40. _____ 1061d

41. (Who's/Whose) the author of this new book on computer technology? (**He** is.)

    41. _____ 1063

42. (Who's/Whose) umbrella is this? (This umbrella is **hers.**)

    42. _____ 1063

F. Directions: Circle the errors in the use of pronouns in the following sentences, and write the correct pronoun forms in the answer column. If a sentence is correct as given, write *C* in the answer column. **References:** ¶¶1061–1063.

43. You can give all of my business management textbooks to whomever wants them.

        43. _____ 1061c

44. Whom do you think will be nominated for vice president at the forthcoming convention?

        44. _____ 1061c

45. Whom shall I say is interested in seeing the Watson property?

        45. _____ 1061c

46. Who did you say you ran into yesterday?

        46. _____ 1061d

47. Whom would you like to speak with today?

        47. _____ 1061d

48. She's the person who I want to hire as Mark Halston's replacement.

        48. _____ 1061d

49. Who's idea was it to double-space all the tables in this manuscript?

        49. _____ 1063

50. Who's the main speaker at the fund-raiser you're holding on Friday night?

        50. _____ 1063

G. Directions: Edit the following paragraph to correct any errors in the use of pronouns. Use appropriate proofreaders' marks to indicate your corrections. Circle any changes you make. **References:** Consult the appropriate rules in ¶¶1049–1063 as you complete this exercise.

```
Just between you and I, I've been seeing a family therapist      1
lately. The fact is, our teenage sons and daughters are driving  2
my husband and me crazy. The therapist says that, among other    3
things, Peter and me have to establish some clear guidelines for 4
the use of our two cars. However, its not a job that Peter and   5
myself look forward to. The first task will be deciding whom      6
gets to use the cars each night. The problem is this: everybody   7
thinks his needs for transportation always have the highest       8
priority. Then theirs the question of whose going to pay for      9
gas. Gina and Kathy are willing to contribute, but neither       10
Craig nor Brad thinks it's their responsibility. I wish I could  11
get some good advice from whomever has successfully dealt with   12
this problem.                                                    13
```

19 Other Grammar Problems

A. Directions: Select the correct form in parentheses in each of the following sentences, and write your answer in the answer column. **References:** Consult the rules shown below as you complete this exercise. See Appendix D for the definition of any grammatical terms that you may not be familiar with.

1. We had a (real, really) nice time at the Abramowitz party on Saturday night.

    1. _____ 1065

2. We were hurt very (bad, badly) by the increases in oil prices in the international market.

    2. _____ 1066

3. We felt very (bad, badly) about the way your departure from the company was handled by the media.

    3. _____ 1067

4. I looked (careful, carefully) at all the statistical analyses you provided before making a decision.

    4. _____ 1067

5. We don't want to come (late, lately) to the reception for the Australian ambassador.

    5. _____ 1068a

6. You need to play (fair, fairly) with all your investors and not just the heavy hitters.

    6. _____ 1068c

7. I drive (faster, more fast) than my son (and that's much too fast).

    7. _____ 1071a

8. I thought it was the (terriblest, most terrible) film that I had ever seen.

    8. _____ 1071c

9. He's feeling (better, more better), now that the effects of his operation have subsided.

    9. _____ 1071d–e

10. Although everyone in my family came down with the flu, my symptoms were the (baddest, worst).

    10. _____ 1071e

B. Directions: Edit the following sentences to correct the errors in grammar. Use appropriate proofreaders' marks (shown on pages 358–359 and on the inside back cover of *The Gregg Reference Manual*) to indicate your corrections. Circle any changes you make. If a sentence is correct as given, write *C* in the answer column. **References:** ¶¶1071–1073.

11. Of the two candidates, we think that Harkavy is the best person for the job.

    11. _____ 1071g

12. Of all the remedies that people suggested, yours seemed to work better.

    12. _____ 1071g

13. Of all the remedies that people suggested, yours seemed to work better than anyone else's.

    13. _____ 1071h

14. Philadelphia is larger than any city in the commonwealth of Pennsylvania.

    14. _____ 1071h

15. My partner, Margaret Costanza, is more productive than anyone in the office.

    15. _____ 1071h

16. This month's sales in the Western Region were 22 percent higher than last month.

    16. _____ 1071i

17. I have almost saved $5000 for the down payment on a new pickup.

    17. _____ 1072

Name _____ Date _____ Class _____ 51

18. When will the cost-benefit analyses of a new water filtration system be finished up? **18.** _____1073_____

19. Let's continue on to fund the research study on air pollution for another six months. **19.** _____1073_____

20. I believe that our best strategy now is to return back to our core business. **20.** _____1073_____

C. Directions: First read ¶¶1074–1075 carefully. Then edit the following sentences to eliminate double negatives. Use appropriate proofreaders' marks to indicate your corrections. Circle any changes you make. **References:** Consult the rules shown below as you complete this exercise.

21. The board members have not accused no one on this panel of conflict of interest. 1076a

22. I have not been able to find nothing wrong with this spreadsheet software. 1076a

23. No one on the Executive Committee likes neither reorganization plan. 1076b

24. I don't have the time nor the patience to listen to Beverly Hellman's problems. 1076c

25. There is no rhyme nor reason to Mr. Honeycutt's new compensation policy. 1076c

D. Directions: If any of the boldface words or phrases are incorrectly used in the following items, write the correct form in the answer column. If an item is correct as given, write *C* in the answer column. **References:** ¶¶1077–1080.

26. How does your new summer home in Maine compare **to** the one you used to own in New Hampshire? **26.** _____ 1077

27. I'm afraid that this copy does not correspond **with** the material I gave you. **27.** _____ 1077

28. The manager of the Reprographics Department maintains that this copy conforms **to** the original. **28.** _____ 1077

29. I've just learned that my salary increase is retroactive **from** January 1. **29.** _____ 1077

30. If you're free for lunch next Wednesday, let's plan to meet **at about** noon. **30.** _____ 1078

31. If you're coming to see Ralph Featherstone, you'll find that his office is **opposite to** mine. **31.** _____ 1078

32. If I can get a 25 percent discount, I'd be willing to order a **couple** cases. **32.** _____ 1079

33. You may disagree with me, but I don't like that **type** design. **33.** _____ 1079

34. The company plans to launch this year's models with extensive ads on TV, **radio,** and in magazines. **34.** _____ 1079

35. As if our problems weren't already bad enough, we now have something new to worry **about.** **35.** _____ 1080

Other Grammar Problems (Continued)

E. Directions: Rewrite the following sentences to correct all errors in sentence structure. **References:** Consult the rules shown below as you complete this exercise.

36. I thought your article was thought-provoking, insightful, and it was well balanced in its approach. _____

_____

_____ 1081a

37. Ann Rowe is not only a talented writer, but she is also a skillful photographer. _____

_____

_____ 1081b

38. Having now completed a review of your manuscript, some questions need to be raised. _____

_____

_____ 1082a

39. To get more information about our products, this toll-free number should be called. _____

_____

_____ 1082b

40. In testing this database management program, a number of bugs were found by our staff. _____

_____

_____ 1082c

41. If purchased by July 1, alterations will be made on these suits at no charge. _____

_____

_____ 1082d

42. I saw two cars collide in the parking lot while racing for the train. _____

_____

_____ 1082
1083

43. As the main speaker at our convention, we feel that you should focus on the issues that most concern you. _____

_____

_____ 1082
1084a

44. This memo contains some valuable advice on how to protect your computer files from our technical experts on staff. _____

_____

_____ 1082
1086

45. A woman's wallet was reported stolen from her desk by the head of our corporate security department. _____

_____

_____ 1082
1086

F. Directions: Edit the following paragraph to correct any errors in grammar. Use appropriate proofreaders' marks to indicate your corrections. Circle any changes you make. **References:** Consult the appropriate rules in ¶¶1065–1088 as you complete this exercise.

I'm not what you would call a decisive type person. Last   1

week I thought I had found a real nice van. It was only two   2

years old, very well equipped, and it had less than 20,000 miles   3

on it. I spotted another van that is almost identical with the   4

one I saw last week while I was driving to work today. It has a   5

much better sound system compared to the first van, but is it   6

really worth the extra money? I honestly can't decide which one   7

I like best. My brother Joe is more knowledgeable about cars   8

than anyone in my family. I've asked him for advice, but I've   9

not heard nothing from him so far. I do need a new set of   10

wheels very bad, but maybe I should wait for a few months on   11

the chance that next year's prices will be lower than this   12

year. Who knows?   13

20 Usage

A. Directions: Select the correct form in parentheses in each of the following sentences, and write it in the answer column. **References:** Section 11, pages 311–332, of *The Gregg Reference Manual.* The individual entries are listed alphabetically. If you have difficulty finding an entry, consult the list at the start of Section 11 (on pages 308–310).

1. Jan has made (a, an) unreasonable request for time off this month.

2. Environmental pollution is (a, an) universal problem that affects us all.

3. Thanks (alot, allot, a lot) for your help on the Farnsworth project.

4. I (accidently, accidentally) dropped the keys to your car somewhere in the parking lot.

5. My brother Sylvester is (adverse, averse) to getting up before ten o'clock.

6. The new legislation has had little (affect, effect) on our business operations.

7. Will stricter regulations (affect, effect) the way we deal with our distributors?

8. The new CEO has (affected, effected) a big change in the number of middle management positions.

9. Christopher D'Alessandro, (age, aged) 11, is already a champion tennis player.

10. A large (amount, number) of voters turned down the proposal for a new stadium.

11. We will (appraise, apprise) you of any new developments in the hearings.

12. Marsha felt very (bad, badly) about your decision to take another job.

13. Timothy stood (beside, besides) me when I really needed advice and support.

14. The Blumenthal estate will be divided (between, among) the three grandchildren.

15. Terry (don't, doesn't) understand why I am so angry about her comments.

16. I drove a hundred miles (farther, further) yesterday than I had intended.

17. We have received (fewer, less) complaints about our service this year.

18. Frank was (indifferent, in different) to the recommendations that Joan offered him.

19. As a rule, I (lay, lie) down every afternoon for a thirty-minute nap.

20. Yesterday afternoon I (lay, laid) down and slept for more than two hours.

1. _____
2. _____
3. _____
4. _____
5. _____
6. _____
7. _____
8. _____
9. _____
10. _____
11. _____
12. _____
13. _____
14. _____
15. _____
16. _____
17. _____
18. _____
19. _____
20. _____

B. Directions: If any of the boldface words or phrases are incorrectly used in the following items, write the correct form in the answer column. If an item is correct as given, write *C* in the answer column. **References:** Section 11, pages 311–332.

21. Do you think **a** FBI investigation is warranted in a case of this type?

21. _____

22. What sort **a** tasks are involved in this software development project?

22. _____

23. My partners and I have taken an **averse** view of Jefferson's invitation to join his firm.

23. _____

24. We're convinced that everything will be **alright** once we get a new CEO.

24. _____

25. I want to reassure you that the first draft of the quarterly report is **all most** completed.

25. _____

26. Everything was supposed to be **already** to be shipped last Friday.

26. _____

27. It's been **all together** too long since the four of us have gotten together.

27. _____

28. We need to explore **all ways** in which we can boost our sales and profits.

28. _____

29. We're very **anxious** to get started on the market research and the field tests.

29. _____

30. I certainly won't do business with that wholesaler **any more.**

30. _____

31. I will be glad to reschedule our meeting at **anytime** in the future.

31. _____

32. You can have the office decorated and furnished **anyway** you want.

32. _____

33. I will personally **assure** that the work is completed according to your specifications.

33. _____

34. Samantha has decided to postpone her trip to the Middle East for **awhile.**

34. _____

35. I think you **better** tone down your reply to Ed's memo.

35. _____

36. Isn't it strange that the sketches done by Ron and Steve are **both alike?**

36. _____

Usage (Continued)

37. I don't doubt **but what** she'll be promoted to executive vice president.

37. _____

38. I **couldn't hardly** understand what Fred was suggesting at the board meeting.

38. _____

39. A visit by the President is not an **every day** occurrence in our town.

39. _____

40. The general manager notified everyone **except Val and I** about the company's plans to relocate.

40. _____

41. I will not **graduate** college until I rewrite my senior thesis and have it accepted.

41. _____

42. When the CEO asked you to sharpen the focus of your proposal, he wanted you to **hone** in on a competitive analysis.

42. _____

43. Are you **inferring** that Marshall Estabrook lied on the witness stand?

43. _____

44. Paul just flew **into** visit his parents during the Christmas holidays.

44. _____

45. I'm writing **in regards to** your fax of June 2, in which you requested our proposal.

45. _____

46. We have not been **indirect** contact with Helen Morrison for over a year.

46. _____

47. The new process **insures** that customers will receive faster service.

47. _____

48. **Irregardless** of what you think, I intend to reorganize the division.

48. _____

49. My wife and I have never cared much for those **kind** of movies.

49. _____

50. Who made off with the printouts that were **laying** on top of my desk?

50. _____

C. Directions: Rewrite the following sentences to correct all errors in usage. Some (but not all) of the errors appear in boldface. **References:** Section 11, pages 311–332.

51. **Incidently,** the large amount of orders that came in yesterday have all ready been processed. _____
_____

52. **Additionally,** I would **appreciate** if you would write once in **awhile** to keep me appraised of any new developments. _____
_____

53. I just applied to a HMO that is supposed to be **equally as good** as the one I currently belong to, but I have received no response, **however.**_____
_____

54. **Firstly,** you will need to demonstrate your proficiency in languages such as Japanese, Chinese, Korean, **etc.** _____
_____

55. I doubt **if** the plane will take off on schedule **due to** the averse weather conditions at the airport. ____
_____

56. Fran was supposed to arrive **at about** 10 o'clock. **Being that** the traffic is backed up for miles, I **doubt** that she will arrive before noon._____
_____

57. Between you and I, I was **kind of** surprised that Tim **enthused over** the architect's sketches._____
_____

58. **In regards to** the **last** version of the agenda for tomorrow's meeting, I left a copy laying on your desk.
_____

59. The attorneys are anxious to assure that the two companies do not sue **one another.**_____
_____

60. Please do not schedule anymore meetings for me this week, **as** I am already overcommitted._____
_____

D. Directions: Edit the following paragraph to correct any errors in usage. Use appropriate proofreaders' marks (shown on pages 358–359 and on the inside back cover of *The Gregg Reference Manual*) to indicate your corrections. Circle any changes you make. **References:** Section 11, pages 311–332.

If our computer training program is moved to the school in Fall Brook,	1
alot of us would be seriously effected. I would have to drive at least five	2
miles further to school, and many students beside me would have to spend	3
all together too much time everyday traveling back and forth. Ms. Gray, the	4
program director, enthused over the advantages of moving the program, but I	5
couldn't hardly understand her reasoning. I seriously doubt that the move	6
will really take place, but I know that I'll feel very badly if it does.	7

21 Usage (Continued)

A. Directions: Select the correct form in parentheses in each of the following sentences, and write it in the answer column. **References:** Section 11, pages 332–345, of *The Gregg Reference Manual.* The individual entries are listed alphabetically. If you have difficulty finding an entry, consult the list at the start of Section 11 (on pages 308–310).

1. I was (learned, taught) by someone who is an expert in spreadsheet software. 1. _____

2. (Leave, Let) me see whether your notes from the conference agree with mine. 2. _____

3. It now looks (like, as if) the storm will last through the entire weekend. 3. _____

4. (Like, As) I said before, I can't get authorization to travel for the rest of the year. 4. _____

5. (May, Can) I speak with you next week about my request for a six-month leave of absence? 5. _____

6. What advertising (media, medium) does the most to increase your sales? 6. _____

7. Bret must (of, have) been the one who spread the story about the Mertzes. 7. _____

8. Am I to believe that this Waterford pitcher just rolled (off, off of) the table by itself? 8. _____

9. Sue was (real, really) disappointed that you couldn't be present at her party. 9. _____

10. I'll call (someday, some day) next week to try to set up a lunch date. 10. _____

11. Let's meet (sometime, some time) soon to review all the alternatives we have. 11. _____

12. We managed to spend (sometime, some time) together at the convention last month. 12. _____

13. Weren't you (supposed, suppose) to notify the media about our plans to relocate? 13. _____

14. I can (sure, surely) use some good advice about which printer to buy. 14. _____

15. You need to take another (tack, tact) with Henry if you want him to change his mind. 15. _____

16. Today's performance came off much better (than, then) yesterday's. 16. _____

17. My husband and I (used to, use to) take a two-mile walk every day. 17. _____

18. I'm afraid that all of us here are caught in a vicious (circle, cycle). 18. _____

19. It's a long (way, ways) from northern New Hampshire to southern California. 19. _____

20. I (would have, would of) been glad to help you if only you had asked me. 20. _____

Name _____ Date _____ Class _____   59

B. Directions: If any of the boldface words or phrases are incorrectly used in the following items, write the correct form in the answer column. If an item is correct as given, write *C* in the answer column. **References:** Section 11, pages 332–345.

21. I have a nosy neighbor who claims that she can **literally** hear the grass grow.

21. _____

22. Jennifer's company **maybe** sending her to an international sales conference in Singapore.

22. _____

23. **Most all** our clients are self-employed, and many of them work out of their homes.

23. _____

24. Please ask your guests not to drive **on to** our lawn.

24. _____

25. After the Butterfield case Victoria went **onto** do bigger and better things.

25. _____

26. Please be sure to follow **upon** Sid's progress on a regular basis.

26. _____

27. I look **up on** my grades for this semester as a total disaster.

27. _____

28. Only a small **percent** of the voters favored the two propositions on the ballot.

28. _____

29. What was the **principle** reason for our loss of market share?

29. _____

30. Mrs. Butterworth told me that she is **reticent** to file a complaint with the commission.

30. _____

31. Ask all visitors to **sit** their luggage down in the reception room closet.

31. _____

32. I thought I made it clear that no one except me was to use **this here** computer.

32. _____

33. The windows behind my desk look out **towards** the Washington Monument.

33. _____

34. I think we should **try and** negotiate a better price for these supplies.

34. _____

35. If the sale of the Kastendorf property goes through, Joe and I will **divide up** the profits equally.

35. _____

Usage (Continued)

C. Directions: Rewrite the following sentences to correct all errors in usage. Some (but not all) of the errors appear in boldface. **References:** Section 11, pages 332–345.

36. **More importantly,** you should of brought the problem to my attention sometime ago._____

_____

_____

37. The **reason** for the delay in processing telephone orders **is because** we are still not use to the new procedures._____

_____

_____

38. It was sure nice of you to learn me how to use **these kind** of spreadsheet applications. _____

_____

_____

39. **Per your request,** I will try and set up a luncheon with Ross Potter for someday next week. _____

_____

_____

40. Can I borrow your lecture notes this weekend like we agreed last Wednesday? _____

_____

_____

41. I need to catch upon the latest developments in the Cavatelli case, **plus** I need to report **same** to the members of the board._____

_____

_____

42. **Who ever** prepared this analysis **doesn't scarcely** understand why our company is in so much trouble profit**wise.** _____

_____

_____

43. Be **sure and** remind the staff that we must all do a better job of **servicing** our clients **then** we have in the past. _____

_____

_____

44. If the customer's claim about scalding soup is valid, it looks like we are literally in the soup ourselves.

_____

_____

45. After our stay in Chicago, we maybe traveling onto Fort Worth and Albuquerque. _____

_____

_____

D. Directions: Edit the following paragraph to correct any errors in usage. Use appropriate proofreaders' marks (shown on pages 358–359 and on the inside back cover of *The Gregg Reference Manual*) to indicate your corrections. Circle any changes you make. **References:** Section 11, pages 332–345.

```
    I'm not real happy about the decision to leave the vice          1

president appoint who ever flatters her to a managerial              2

position. It would be more appropriate to let the entire com-        3

mittee share in this kind of decision, like we have done in the      4

past. I suppose I should of raised an objection at our last          5

meeting, but I guess I wasn't thinking very clearly than. I'm        6

surprised that nobody else raised any objection, because we use      7

to make these sort of decisions as a group. I don't scarcely        8

know what action to take now, plus it may be too late to over-       9

turn the vice president's action.                                   10
```

Basic Worksheets on
Grammar, Usage, and Style for
The Gregg Reference Manual
Tenth Edition

A. Directions: Rewrite the following sentences to correct all errors in grammar and usage. **References:** Consult the appropriate rules in Sections 10–11 as you complete this exercise.

1. Schuyler and myself use to work on the Phillips case, but one of the other lawyers have been handling it alone for sometime now. _____

2. Phyllis *says* that she is real sorry for what she done, but if she *was* sorry, she would of apologized much more fast than she did. _____

3. None of the department managers has given Sharon and I the expense projections that we need to finish up the budget analyses. _____

4. Between you and I, it looks like our contract negotiations with Jim Fortunato has broke down all together. _____

5. The number of new subscriptions have rose alot faster than any of us could have foreseen. _____

6. Mrs. Abernathy, the person who's car I accidently backed into, maybe adverse to settling her claim for damages out of court. _____

_____

_____

7. If Mr. Pendleton is inferring that the products of our competitors are better than our's, he obviously don't know that we get a lot less complaints from purchasers than they do. _____

_____

_____

8. My partners and me plan to wait for awhile before we go any farther with our plans to take over the Kendall Corporation and reinvest it's assets. _____

_____

_____

9. I feel very badly about him deciding to return back to his old job when he had all ready done such good work for us. _____

_____

_____

10. There was so many good reasons why the jury were suppose to rule against the defendant that neither the judge nor the lawyers was expecting a hung jury. _____

_____

_____

Editing Survey C (Continued)

B. Directions: Edit the following paragraphs to correct all errors. Use appropriate proofreaders' marks (shown on pages 358–359 and on the inside back cover of *The Gregg Reference Manual*) to indicate your corrections. Circle any changes you make. **References:** Consult the appropriate rules in Sections 1–11 as you complete this exercise.

```
    There are still some Bostonians who consider their city the          1

center of the world.  One of my father-in-laws' favorite stories        2

concerns a European traveller arriving at Boston's Logan Airport        3

in mid-December sometime back in the 70's.  Coming out of the           4

airport, an empty cab was waiting to take him to his hotel in           5

the City. As they drove along the passenger asked the driver           6

whether he could recommend some sights that a first time visitor        7

to Boston should see.                                                   8

    "Alright," said the driver. "Let's see. You certainly              9

ought to visit our great universitys--Harvard and M.I.T.--and at       10

this time of year you ought to go to the planetarium. There is         11

an exhibit showing how the stars were arranged in the sky on the       12

night that Jesus was born."                                            13

    "Over Bethlehem?" asked the visitor.                               14

    "No," said the driver with some exasperation. "Over Bos-           15

ton, of course."                                                       16
```

C. Directions: Edit the following paragraphs to correct all errors. Use appropriate proofreaders' marks to indicate your corrections. Circle any changes you make. **References:** Consult the appropriate rules in Sections 1–11 as you complete this exercise.

There is an exclusive country club located in one of Bos-   1
tons' more affluent suburbs. Its so exclusive that guests who   2
are brought there by members are considered "visitors" if they   3
live within ten miles of the club and "strangers" if they live   4
further away. To approach the club, you drive between imposing   5
stone pillars, you cross part of the golf course, you drive   6
passed a squat, owlish-looking security guard and you come to an   7
oval where all the club facilities are located.   8

On a lovely Spring day--I believe it was in May, 1989--a   9
late-model Mercedes driven by a well dressed man was only one of   10
a large number of cars that streamed past the guard. About an   11
hour after the Mercedes left, the manager of the golf shop dis-   12
covered that while he had been at lunch, someone had broke in   13
and stolen a good deal of sports equipment. When the police   14
came to investigate, the guard urged them to track down the man   15
in the Mercedes. He even supplied them with the license plate   16
number of the car. When the police intercepted the car a short   17
time later, they discovered all of the stolen items in the   18
trunk.   19

The police immediately returned to ask the guard what had   20
made him suspect a well-dressed man in an expensive car. The   21
guard replied, "It was obvious. The man smiled and waved at me   22
as he drove in. I knew at once that he was not a member of the   23
club".   24

23 Final Survey

A. Directions: Correct all errors in punctuation in each of the following items. Use appropriate proofreaders' marks (shown on pages 358–359 and on the inside back cover of *The Gregg Reference Manual*) to indicate your corrections. Circle any changes you make. If an item is correct as given, write *C* in the answer column. **References:** Consult the appropriate rules in Sections 1–2 as you complete this exercise.

1. Will you please sign your name below _____

2. Will you please let me borrow your BMW _____

3. We asked Tim when he planned to retire _____

4. Tim, when are you planning to retire _____

5. You need someone, who writes good ad copy. _____

6. It is, therefore, essential to act now. _____

7. On Friday, May 4 2007 I will be forty years old. _____

8. I can help you paint this weekend but Eileen and Gail have a number of other commitments. _____

9. My lawyer my accountant and I are trying to untangle my tax problems. _____

10. We had a frank open discussion about her work.

11. To get the best service call 555-4825. _____

12. Before you leave make sure that Mr. Thomas gets a copy of your report. _____

13. In my judgment the buyout offer from Chadwick is not worth considering. _____

14. I took your suggestion, and found that it solved the problem. _____

15. Monday and Wednesday are good for me, Friday is not. _____

16. The name Floyd Fowler doesn't ring a bell. _____

17. The dealer's terms seem fair, for example, he's giving you a good price on your car. _____

18. The chapter called Glued to the Tube is one of the best in the book. _____

19. What does the word muffin-choker mean? _____

20. My next book, Second Wind, will be published early next year. _____

B. Directions: Correct the capitalization as necessary in each of the following items. Use appropriate revision marks to indicate your corrections. Circle any changes you make. If an item is correct as given, write *C* in the answer column. **References:** Consult the appropriate rules in Section 3 as you complete this exercise.

21. graduated from Stanford university _____

22. a speech given by the first lady _____

23. must discuss it with my Doctor _____

24. a ruling by the state Attorney General _____

25. an exhibit of my Mother's paintings _____

26. check out of the Hotel by 10 a.m. _____

27. a strong reaction from west side voters _____

28. a surprising trend during the Nineties _____

29. a master's degree in Physical Therapy _____

30. the data shown in Table 4 on page 128 _____

C. Directions: Circle all errors in number style and abbreviations in each of the following items, and write the correct form in the answer column. If an item is correct as given, write *C* in the answer column. **References:** Consult the appropriate rules in Sections 4–5 as you complete this exercise.

31. starting January fifteenth _____

32. a lot more than six percent _____

33. eight lawyers and 12 paralegals _____

34. forty-five thousand dollars _____

35. was priced at $299.00 _____

36. costs only $.79 a dozen _____

37. . . . last year. 12 weeks later . . . _____

38. in the first decade of the 21st century _____

39. more than ¾ of the voters _____

40. will not end until 5:00 p.m. _____

41. Harvey O. Genther Senior _____

42. miles per gallon *(abbreviated)* _____

43. ought to notify the F.B.I. _____

44. hire a temp. for two weeks _____

45. write to M.F. Noonan _____

46. waiting to see Doctor Katzenbach _____

47. the US Treasury Department _____

48. moved to Oberlin, Oh., last year _____

49. 550 lbs. *(on an invoice)* _____

50. discuss it with your Ceo _____

Final Survey (Continued)

D. Directions: Circle all errors dealing with plural and possessive forms, spelling, and compound words in the following items. Write the correct form in the answer column. If an item is correct as given, write *C* in the answer column. **References:** Consult the appropriate rules in Sections 6–8 as you complete this exercise.

51. received four faxs yesterday _____

52. rethink our company policys _____

53. will need three more shelfs _____

54. talked with my two brother-in-laws _____

55. an extraordinary phenomena _____

56. consulted several M.D.'s _____

57. a six month's leave of absence _____

58. talk to the sale's manager _____

59. review the witness' testimony _____

60. a sale on womens' sportswear _____

61. prefered to use my own tools _____

62. offered to pay for the tickets _____

63. we thought it was wholely acceptable _____

64. all of us felt greatly relieved _____

65. exceded the weight limit _____

66. we can not forgo our rights _____

67. sited a recent consumer poll _____

68. in the fourth faze of the project _____

69. planning separate itineries _____

70. ordered a similar quanity _____

71. plan to get-together soon _____

72. form a committee of laymen _____

73. need to spot check her work _____

74. got her training on-the-job _____

75. a cost effective approach _____

76. should be more broad minded _____

77. chose someone not well-known _____

78. to co-ordinate our efforts _____

79. need to re-emphasize that _____

80. a self addressed envelope _____

E. Directions: Circle all errors dealing with grammar and usage in the following items, and write the correct form in the answer column. If an item is correct as given, write *C* in the answer column. **References:** Consult the appropriate rules in Sections 10–11 as you complete this exercise.

81. Bob don't have very much imagination. _____

82. One of my clients are going to sue me. _____

83. We begun this ad campaign on October 1. _____

84. If I was free, I'd go with you. _____

85. Sandy and me have decided to get married. _____

86. The firm has improved it's sales. _____

87. The assignment was given to Doug and myself. _____

88. I feel badly about the way you were treated. _____

89. Which is the best of the two plans? _____

90. Don't tell no one about my idea. _____

91. I planned an European vacation. _____

92. I used to see Paul once in awhile. _____

93. We are already to test the software. _____

94. How will this effect our profits? _____

95. We got a large amount of calls. _____

96. It's more trouble then it's worth. _____

97. Try to express your thoughts in less words. _____

98. Joan should of called by now. _____

99. Fran did a real nice job, didn't she? _____

100. Who is suppose to take your place? _____